Shooting for Excellence

Shooting for Excellence

African American and Youth Culture in
New Century Schools

Jabari Mahiri
University of California at Berkeley

National Council of Teachers of English
1111 W. Kenyon Road, Urbana, Illinois 61801–1096

Teachers College Press
Teachers College, Columbia University
New York & London

Staff Editor: Zarina M. Hock

Interior Design: Tom Kovacs for TGK design

Cover Design: Evelyn C. Shapiro

Cover Photograph © Elizabeth Crews

NCTE Stock Number: 44632–3050

Published simultaneously by the National Council of Teachers of English and Teachers College Press, 1234 Amsterdam Avenue, New York, NY 10027.

Teachers College Press ISBN: 0-8077-3788-7

It is the policy of NCTE in its journals and other publications to provide a forum for the open discussion of ideas concerning the content and the teaching of English and the language arts. Publicity accorded to any particular point of view does not imply endorsement by the Executive Committee, the Board of Directors, or the membership at large, except in announcements of policy, where such endorsement is clearly specified.

Library of Congress Cataloging–in–Publication Data

Mahiri, Jabari.
    Shooting for excellence: African American and youth culture in new century schools/Jabari Mahiri.
        p.   cm.
    Includes bibliographical references (p.   ) and index.
    "NCTE stock number: 44632-3050"—T.p. verso.
    ISBN 0-8141-4463-2
    1. Language and education—United States. 2. Afro-Americans—Education. 3.Afro-Americans—Education (Secondary) 4. Popular culture—United States. 5. Multicultural education—United States. 6. Educational anthropology—United States. 7. English language—Study and teaching—Afro-American students. 8. Language and education—United States.
I. Title.
LC2717.M35 1998
373.182996'073—dc21   98-7066
                                                            CIP

To Nia and Ayana
twin inspirations
&
To son-men
Kobie and Jelani

Contents

1 Introduction: The Challenge of African American and Youth Culture in Changing Schools

A teacher in one of my research projects—an elegant African American woman who has been a successful, urban high school English teacher of mostly African American and Latino students for more than twenty years—thinly conceals her exasperation as she struggles to apprehend why she is not being as successful with the students currently enrolled in her classes. Though they arrive at school and click off their stereo headphones resonating reggae, rock, and hip-hop, their rhythms of learning seem out of sync with a cadence of teaching that has worked well for her in the past. She has always seen herself as a catalyst for her students, enhancing the quality of their critical thinking and improving their learning skills. Now she has begun to reflect on ways to change herself and her teaching strategies in order to be more effective with this generation of students.

This teacher's situation reflects one aspect of the challenges in education today, faced by both teachers and students. Increasingly, we see that despite numerous reform initiatives to change schools, many teachers are increasingly frustrated in their attempts to reach and teach contemporary students. At the high school level, cycles of reform have continued for over one hundred years since the "Committee of Ten" first considered issues of secondary schooling in a national context in the early 1890s (Evans & Walker, 1966). One of the committee's recommendations—that English be required for a minimum of five hours a week for all four years—helped to establish the prominence of English in high school curricula to this day. The prominence of this subject in schools, along with the critical and ideological issues surrounding the current focus on literacy development (especially regarding marginalized groups), makes considerations and reforms for teaching and learning English particularly crucial. These issues become just as crucial in a global context, where the extensive use of English as an official or unofficial language in over sixty countries is inextricably linked to influences of imperialism and cultural domination, past and present. [1]

Among all the reform initiatives and other changes affecting the school-place, however, there is also a pervasive sense that the students themselves have dramatically changed. They are the MTV generation.

More than half of the 27.5 million teenagers in the United States own their own television sets; they have significant buying power, having spent $100 billion in 1993 alone, a 30 percent increase over 1989 (Tully, "The Universal Teenager," *Fortune* magazine, 1994). They make more choices independent of their parents about the music they listen to, how they dress, where they go, and who they "hang out" with. Also, more than ever before, they come from single-parent homes. Many don't have a sense of physical security; they worry about gang violence and AIDS, and they commit suicide in record numbers.

The teacher in my research project acknowledged that she was not aware enough of the day-to-day realities in her students' lives, and she has not even been able to rely on her shared ethnic identity with her students to enhance her effectiveness in teaching them. They often question, resist, or reject the school knowledge that she has been positioned and sanctioned to teach. Some students do this consciously and aggressively through overt, oppositional behavior, but their attitude is also manifested in more subtle behaviors that seem to reflect a disaffection from learning.

Positionality of Students and Teachers

Signithia Fordham and John Ogbu (1986) make the case that African American culture itself is oppositional to the culture of schools. They argue that African American students associate school knowledge and official school culture with "acting white" and see this as a violation of their identification with fictive kinship norms. Bracha Alpert (1991) studied English classes in a suburban high school and argues that life in these kinds of classrooms contained significant resistance behaviors also. He noted that student resistance was linked to the teaching approach. He found that resistance was more likely to occur when the teachers' primary emphasis in the classroom was academic subject-matter; and acceptance was more likely when students' personal knowledge was incorporated into instruction in conjunction with a responsive style of classroom discourse.

The Fordham and Ogbu formulation suggests that the oppositional nature of African American culture in relationship to school culture is relatively fixed, based on a historically structured and enforced "castelike" position of subordination and on a perception of conflicts between the norms of their (African American) fictive kinship system and the value as well as values of schools and the larger society. But this conception of school culture does not incorporate a critique of the role of schools as an extension of the societal structures that dominate and marginalize African American students and other groups. Instead, Fordham and Ogbu view schools as embodying meritocratic liberal ideology. Consequently, they imply that it is the nature of African American culture rather than the nature of school culture that must be changed.

Alpert's formulation allows for more flexibility in the motives for resistance by suggesting that students' responses of either resistance or acceptance are at least in part predicated on the specific nature of pedagogy and curriculum to which they are exposed. From this perspective, student resistance to school culture can be a focal point for developing ways to change school culture so that it serves both the lives and learning of students. It must be clear, however, that not all of the oppositional behavior of students constitutes real resistance. Henry Giroux (1983) notes that behavior is only resistant to the degree that it "promotes critical thinking and reflective action and contains the possibility of galvanizing collective political struggle" (p. 3).

Teachers, as well as parents and school administrators, need to continue to change the way they both perceive of and participate in schooling. They need to become sources of resistance themselves to the ideology and practices of cultural domination and exploitation that permeate institutional structures in this society, including its schools. One way teachers can do this is by working to better understand and to build on the authentic experiences of students who have been marginalized in and by the educational process through the creation of what Joao Viegas Fernandes (1988) calls counter-hegemonic curricula. He notes that rather than being mere instruments of propaganda, teachers can be internal sources of resistance and that counter-hegemonic curricula should be seen as internal mechanisms of resistance. Fernandes cautions that it "is necessary to take into account whether the direction of the main resultant leads to resistance against ideological inculcation or to reinforcement of the dominant ideology" (p. 175).

An important aspect of Fernandes's notion of teachers as internal sources of resistance is also addressed by bell hooks in *Teaching to Transgress* (1994). She extends the focus from students to teachers in a call for teachers to create "engaged pedagogy." She argues that the kind of dialogue and introspection needed for transformative learning can only occur when teachers themselves are working toward self-actualization in conjunction with their attempts for authentic engagement with students. Engaged pedagogies, says bell hooks, motivate both teachers and students to unmask the workings of authoritative discourses and to see how various sources of knowledge are either sanctioned or subjugated.

An additional consideration for engaged pedagogies stems from the fact that teachers in American schools are increasingly finding that they are teaching "other people's children." For example, the reality of many

African American students, especially in the nation's urban public schools, is that though they are in classroom settings that are overwhelmingly populated by other African American students, more and more they are being educated by teachers from cultures other than their own. The National Center for Education Information reported in 1996 that nearly 90 percent of U. S. teachers are white and that "Even in urban schools, which have a high proportion of minority students, 73 percent of teachers identify themselves as white" (*San Francisco Chronicle*, October 17, 1996, A2). As Gloria Ladson-Billings cogently argues in *The Dreamkeepers* (1994), these considerations along with the general trends toward even greater diversity, make it all the more important for the implementation of effective instructional strategies that do not depend on the race or ethnicity of the teacher. In order to be effective, teachers will need to become more aware of their own positionality in American culture, even as they increase their awareness of and sensitivity to the diverse backgrounds, orientations, and interests of their students.

More work is needed to further clarify the historically defined and institutionally structured forces that surround and influence classroom practices. However, I will attempt to show how teachers already have considerable agency to transform key aspects of schooling by instituting classroom curricula and teaching practices that can help students to more clearly understand, effectively negotiate, and ultimately critique and change the sociocultural, economic, and political conditions that contextualize and often constrain their lives and learning. Recent reform movements are well-intentioned, but Roland Tharp and Ronald Gallimore (1988) note that such movements often do not define specific teaching practices in the classroom nor do they provide additional means through which teachers can actually improve.

I draw on findings and implications from four research projects to suggest ways that classroom discourse, curricula, and culture can be changed to enhance processes of teaching and learning by building more powerfully on authentic experiences of students. Although these suggestions are primarily directed toward high school English and college writing classrooms, I believe there are also transformative implications for other levels and subjects as well.

A Role for African American and Youth Culture

African American culture has been given a central focus in this discussion. It is not that it should have a privileged place vis-à-vis other cultural groups. However, illuminating the viability and significance of black difference is a key way of making the issue of difference significant in

U.S. schools. African American culture also has generative links to popular youth culture and therefore offers one window into understanding
youth generally. Increasingly alien to adults, youth popular culture is
becoming amazingly uniform in a global community of young people
who listen to the same music, wear the same clothes, play the same video
games, and emulate the same heroes. The links between African American and youth culture are not limited to areas such as music and sports,
where black achievements and styles set world standards of excellence.
They are pervasive in other aspects of culture as well and are reflected
in ways of thinking, ways of behaving, and ways of being.

This pervasiveness has, in fact, caused some white parents to complain about an Afro-Americanization of their children. The issue was
epitomized in a situation that occurred at North Newton Junior-Senior
High School near Morocco, Indiana, when two sisters and about fifteen
others "stylized" themselves by braiding their hair and wearing the kinds
of baggy clothes popular with black youth. E. Jean Carroll described the
resulting tensions that occurred in the town between adults and these
youth (and between these youth and other youth) in an *Esquire* article
(1994) alluding to Norman Mailer's *The White Negro* (1957). Interestingly,
Carroll, a white woman, consciously used a number of images and styles
from black language and culture, especially the practice of signifying, to
depict this town. She wrote, "It's . . . the point where the farm belt, the
Bible belt, and the rust belt intersect and the women are so homely that
even the big-legged coeds of Purdue, famed nationwide for their ugli-
ness and surliness, look like prom queens in comparison" (p. 102). One
of the main points from the article was that these youth understood and
were trying to escape the elemental boredom and sameness in their lives
by embracing and reflecting youth cultural behaviors and styles drawn
from the influences of rap and hip-hop.

Youth popular culture, however, should not be essentialized as a distinct entity unto itself which can then be neatly informed or transformed
by other cultural agents. Youth are not a subgroup separate from adults;
they are always in dynamic, reciprocally influencing interactions as they
move inside and between multiple, variegated contexts. Ralph Cintron
(1993) points out the permeability and instability of notions of boundaries within and between communities, which complicate attempts to
distinctly package any particular cultural grouping. Drawing on Mikhail
Bakhtin (1986), he calls attention to how communities inter-animate each
other through contact that results in continual exchanges of values, behaviors, and beliefs. So, rather than seeing African American or youth
cultural constructs statically, recognition is given to how their fluid and
mutable qualities can contribute to the play of difference and change in
society and, as I want to argue, in schools.

In *The Black Atlantic* (1993), Paul Gilroy explicates the embeddedness of black experiences in the developments of the modern world. This framework is also useful for exploring how intricately and co-dependently youth popular culture is embedded in contemporary Western and global cultures. A number of scholars, in fact, have provided critiques of embeddedness, rather than mere binary oppositions, of cultural systems engaging each other. In critiquing contemporary multiculturalism in "Beyond the Culture Wars: Identities in Dialogue," for example, Henry Louis Gates Jr.(1993) argues for a perspective that shifts the focus away from just the delineation of differences between groups to the ways that group identity is dynamically constructed and positioned within historical, political, and socioeconomic contexts. In a more recent article (1995) he reminds us of Ralph Ellison's early "insistence on the Negro's centrality to American culture" (p. 62). In "The New Cultural Politics of Difference," Cornel West (1990) notes that the United States through its emergence as a world power has taken center stage in the worldwide production and circulation of culture, and in so doing it has also facilitated a movement away from traditional high culture toward mainstream American popular culture. So relationships between African American and U. S. culture can clearly and quickly have global influences.

In "What Is This 'Black' in Black Popular Culture?" Stuart Hall (1993) critiques the possibilities (and problems) of black popular culture in terms of its potential to make a difference with respect to shifting the dispositions of power. Hall writes, "In its expressivity, its musicality, its orality, in its rich, deep, and varied attention to speech, in its inflections toward the vernacular and the local, in its rich production of counter-narratives, and above all, in its metaphorical use of the musical vocabulary, black popular culture has enabled the surfacing, inside the mixed and contradictory modes even of some mainstream popular culture, of elements of a discourse that is different—other forms of life, other traditions of representation" (p. 109). This sentence captures key aspects of the viability and significance of black difference that I believe can be built upon to make a difference in schools. In the studies reported in subsequent chapters, I attempt to show how contexts for teaching and learning can, in fact, honor and draw on elements of both cultural and personal differences of students by utilizing elements from African American communicative and cultural styles in the classroom.

A recurring feature in African American discourse and culture—the quality of motion—is reflected in the term "shooting." This quality of rapid motion is seen in many expressions like "shootin' the breeze," "shootin' the bull," "shootin' twenty feet of j-ism." Clearly, a different quality of motion is needed in initiatives for school reform, but motion nevertheless. Using "shooting" in the title of this book is congruent with my desire to harness a different quality of motion and changing its aim in much the same way that the book's overall focus is toward harnessing some of the power of African American and youth discourse and culture and focusing it for productive use in schools. I understand how many of the more visible school reform initiatives have appropriated the use of the term "excellence." But, as Mike Rose (1995) notes in *Possible Lives*, "we operate with inadequate, even damaging notions of what it means to be 'excellent'" (p. 3). I don't want to lose sight of goals for excellence, but I want to illustrate alternative paths that permit elbow room for varied cultural and participatory styles as well as more mediums and strategies for representing knowledge.

Ultimately, a key premise of this book is the possibility for more shareable cultural worlds reflective of Toni Morrison's critique of this idea in *Playing in the Dark* (1992). The idea is intricately linked to notions of excellence that encompass equality as well as quality. I argue that aspects of popular youth culture can act as unifying and equalizing forces in culturally diverse classrooms and that African American and youth cultural sources for curricula can motivate learning of traditional subject matter as well. Through the research presented, I explore how some teachers make viable connections between streets and schools to create more shareable cultural worlds for learning.

I begin by looking at a program for youth development that takes place in a setting outside of school. In Chapter 2, I present an ethnographic study completed in 1992 that assessed the language and literacy development of young African American males through interactions with their coaches and other volunteers in a community-based sports program on the South Side of Chicago. The study revealed a number of intriguing literacy activities and significant language competencies that occurred in this sociocultural context outside of school. These community language styles and literacy practices were probed to provide understanding of how some cultural competencies are produced and to lay a foundation for further examining ways to build on these and other youth competencies and interests in schools. As a researcher as well as a former Chicago public school English teacher and college writing instructor, I was interested to see how the discourse strategies and social interactions found to be effective in this out-of-school setting might have potential for increasing the efficacy of teachers in schools.

I subsequently designed and instituted three other research projects presented in Chapters 3, 4, and 5 that explored how classroom teachers could build on features of African American and youth discourse and culture to transform the style and content of classroom discourse and learning. Since these studies were situated in educational settings that were culturally diverse, I also explored how some features from African American and youth discourse and culture could work to help foster cultural understanding and equality between different cultural groups. In Chapter 6, I conclude by synthesizing significant findings and implications from all four studies to set forth a direction for reform and a vision for "New Century Schools" that can incorporate and build on America's cultural diversity to inform and empower students.

Theoretical and Methodological Considerations

The central theoretical considerations that underlie these studies are drawn from the work of Paulo Freire, Mikhail Bakhtin, Lev Vygotsky, Brian Street, Bernardo Ferdman, James Paul Gee, and Thomas Kochman. Key methodological considerations come from the work of Dell Hymes, Shirley Brice Heath, and Courtney Cazden. Conceptual contributions also come from Christina Haas's work on the symbiotic relationship between writing and technology and from Toni Morrison's work on decoding the challenges that blackness presents to American literature and culture in *Playing in the Dark.* Additionally, Theodore Sizer's work (1984) on a coaching model of school reform is significant to these studies.

The metaphor of coaching has gone well beyond the realm of athletics to become a key construct of reformers in education, medicine, and business in their efforts to reshape traditional institutional structures. In education the idea of "teacher as coach," has been used to model a fundamental reorientation of the roles, relationships, and responsibilities of teachers and students. It characterizes an orientation toward teaching and learning that is centered more on active student involvement reflected in code words such as *collaboration, cooperative learning, reciprocal teaching, mentoring, scaffolding, cognitive apprenticeships, peer tutoring and peer response, project-based learning,* and *serious learning games.* Though it cannot be limited to any one reform movement, this metaphor is closely associated with the Coalition of Essential Schools, a national reform movement headed by Sizer. This movement was recently awarded a grant of $50 million to further develop and extend its comprehensive coaching model of teaching.

The Coalition School model clearly addresses the limitations of schooling organized along the lines of a workplace model. In *Horace's Compromise* (1984), Sizer noted that "We talk about 'delivering a service' to students by means of 'instructional strategies'; our metaphors arise from the factory floor and issue from the military manual. . . . [W]hile we know that we don't learn very well that way, nor want very much to have someone else's definition of 'service' to be 'delivered' to us, we accept these metaphors" (p. 3). Sizer's reconceived metaphor for schooling captures part of the dilemma of students positioned as "objects" in the educational process. Yet, the ultimate focus of his reform initiative to improve the general quality of student learning stops short of reconceiving students and reforming education to help empower them in the sense that Freire gives to empowerment as "subjects" with the critical capacity to transform their reality (1970). For Freire, "subjects" know and act while "objects" are known and acted upon. Therefore, beyond the accumulation of information and the development of specific technical skills, learning should be a process of becoming conscious of how one's personal and group experiences are situated within and constructed by particular historical conditions and power relationships. Empowerment, then, is the positioning of "subjects" to challenge and change unequal power relationships. Interestingly, the coaching practices and perspectives in the community sports setting that I observed were not only viable for the development of athletic and academic skills, they also revealed a variety of ways that coaches and other community volunteers attempted to develop these youths as critical and conscious actors in the world beyond sports. This focus on the social development of these youths was designed to both authenticate and significantly expand their experience and perceptions. It attempted to use their desire to effectively engage in sports to help them see possibilities to more effectively engage the world. The sport program's director, formerly a volunteer coach for nine years, summed up this endeavor by saying, "I think we are trying to develop a program here that uses athletics as a way to get to the minds of these youngsters."

In many ways, their goals for these youths were consistent with Freire's notion of the need to move people beyond merely "living" to "existing" in the world, where "existing" for him included development of a critical capacity. So, I focused on the mentoring relationships as well as the language use of both players and coaches in dialogic interactions. I argue that a close examination of the nature of communicative and social interactions that engaged youths in this setting helps to clarify some of the transformative possibilities for teachers as "coaches" engaging students in schools.

I recognize that there are potential problems in using the communicative and social relationship development from this setting to illuminate possibilities for schooling because of the fact that much of the interaction was between men and boys. All too often there has been the tendency to use male-generated or male-dominated models as if they were equally applicable to the issues and situations that females face. This "shortchanging" is particularly pronounced in schooling. For example, The American Association of University Women (AAUW) Report (Style, 1992) notes that "[t]he absence of attention to girls in the current education debate suggests that girls and boys have identical educational experiences in school. Nothing could be further from the truth" (p. 3). Significant findings from the numerous research studies in the AAUW Report reveal how girls have very different experiences and get substantially different treatment while in the same educational settings as boys. Depending upon how it is used, even the metaphor of coaching may privilege males in subtle and not so subtle ways. Yet, I believe that some of the practices and principles revealed in the community sports setting that I assessed can effectively contribute to new styles and strategies for teaching and learning that serve the developmental needs of both girls and boys.

My methodology for assessing language and social interactions in this setting was based in Hymes's work on the ethnography of communication as well as the work of others who have built on Hymes, especially Muriel Saville-Troike. I found that these communicative interactions incorporated a wide range of youth options or "Speaking Rights" that were characterized by being dialogical and receiver-centered, expressive and assertive, playful and colorful, as well as spontaneous and performative. While reflecting important aspects of black language styles as delineated particularly by Kochman, these interactions also revealed the intricate competencies—the on- and off-court *voices*—being developed and reinforced in these youth.

Bakhtin's work gives texture to the social, historical, dialogical, and multivocal qualities of "voice," and it is helpful in understanding why the "Speaking Rights" that facilitate African American youth in finding voice on the courts may have difficulty finding their way into discourse in schools. For Bakhtin, language enters life and life enters language through utterances that constitute the various types of primary and secondary speech genres and reveals the ways that national language is embodied in the language of individuals (1986). He notes that "The very interrelations between primary and secondary genres and the process of the historical formation of the latter shed light on the nature of the utterance (and above all on the complex problem of the interrelations among language, ideology, and world view)." Examination of the dynamic between primary and secondary speech genres, then, can also reveal ways that the voices of some individuals and groups are embodied while others are subjugated in the national language.

In addition to Bakhtin, the theoretical contributions of Vygotsky offer provocative insights into the nature of language, learning, and social development, and some of these insights are applicable to the community sports setting that I studied. Vygotsky's work on relationships between cognition, speech, and social interaction attempted to explain how children develop by appropriating new forms of discourse and thinking through interactions with others. His emphasis on the role of social practice in youth development is important to the discussion of coaching perspectives and practices in the community sports setting as well as to discussions of schooling. In the community sports setting, I show how the coaches' circle operated as a kind of zone of proximal development in which young players appropriated and practiced forms of discourse and thinking through interactions with adult coaches as well as with their peers.

While communicative events were shaped by talk that occurred both inside and outside of the coaches' circle that was primarily the province of men volunteers, literacy events were structured into this sports context by members of the program's parents' council, consisting primarily of women volunteers. As the communicative event as defined by Hymes was the central unit of analysis for language and social practices, the literacy event as defined by Heath (1982) was the central unit of analysis for these literacy practices.

The parents' council organized a number of activities throughout the season, and literacy events were often incorporated into them. But players also engaged in an array of activities on their own, which revealed highly sophisticated, spontaneous and adaptive literacy practices, "Reading Rites," that were tied to personal interests motivated by sports discourse. This was the kind of adaptive learning that Heath and McLaughlin (1987) noted "comes most compellingly through direct need and experience rather than through moral or didactic precepts handed on from others." Both the structured and adaptive literacy practices that occurred in this community sports setting offered insights into competencies predicated on youth experiences that I believe can be connected to new ways of thinking about learning in school.

Brian Street contributes important considerations to a framework for viewing literacy development in the community sports setting as well as in school. In *Literacy in Theory and Practice* (1984) and in *Cross-Cultural Approaches to Literacy* (1993), he debunks the notion of literacy learning having universal consequences for people by illustrating the significance of social institutions and the socialization process in constructing both the meanings and practices for specific cultural groups. He shows how these meanings and practices can and do change dramatically from one social context to another. Consequently, he proposes an "ideological" rather than an "autonomous" model of literacy development. In viewing literacy learning as culturally based, Street calls attention to the fact that people—who they are and how they live—make all the difference in how they will learn and how they will engage in literacy practices.

In an article in the *Harvard Educational Review,* Bernardo Ferdman (1990) adds to Street's framework on the social nature of literacy specific considerations for looking at ways that literacy and culture reciprocally influence each other at the level of the individual. His clear focus on the connections between literacy and culture with respect to the individual learner has direct bearing on how I attempt to draw implications from a cultural model for the literacy learning of individuals in schools. In noting how literacy learning is linked to cultural identity, Ferdman writes that it "both derives from and modulates the symbolic and practical significance of literacy for individuals as well as groups" (p. 182). He defines cultural identity for individuals as the images of behaviors, beliefs, values, and norms that each person maintains as appropriate for members of the ethnic group to which she or he belongs. Ferdman's work poses a key question, and it is useful to see how this book addresses the same question: "How can teachers and other educators better acknowledge their students' cultural identity and consider it in planning and providing more effective literacy education?" (p. 201). James Paul Gee also delineates how literacy learning is culturally based, and his work suggests particular ways that the culturally based styles of language and literacy development in the community sports setting can be related to a model for teaching and learning in schools. In a paper entitled "Learning and Reading: The Situated Sociocultural Mind" (1995), Gee cites extensive work in cognitive science and the philosophy of mind to support a progressively more accepted notion that the human mind is, at root, a *pattern recognizer.* Through citing the work of Nolan (1994), Gee further establishes that in acquiring concepts "learners must have both lots of examples (experience) and must uncover the patterns and sub-patterns in those examples which are the ones explicated by their socioculturally-situated theories." Gee builds from these concepts to show how learning may be specifically "situated" in sociocultural experiences.

> Since the world is infinitely full of potentially meaningful patterns and sub-patterns in any domain, something must guide the learner in selecting which patterns and sub-patterns to focus on. And this something resides in the cultural models of the learner's sociocultural groups and the practices and settings in which they are rooted. *Because* the mind is a pattern recognizer, and there are infinite ways to pattern features of the world, *of necessity,* though perhaps ironi-

cally, the mind *is social* (really *cultural*) in the sense that sociocultural practices and settings guide the patterns in terms of which the
learner thinks, acts, talks, values, and interacts. (p. 3)

Here Gee identifies the significance of cultural models in mediating the
learning of individuals and later notes that this happens in ways that do
not negate individual agency. This mediation of learning is through what
Gee calls midlevel patterns or "representations" that he calls *situated
meanings*. Gee's formulation provides insights into what I believe is key
work for teachers in transforming schools. It involves teachers becoming aware of the situated meanings (the diverse ways of representing)
that students bring to schools and working to understand those situated meanings in terms of the various cultural models that motivate
them as a foundation for student learning. But I also believe teachers
should go beyond this to exposing students to additional situated meanings through engaged pedagogies and counter-hegemonic curricula that
help students to comprehend and critique how the patterns in some
cultural models work either to subjugate or to liberate people, thereby
increasing their consciousness of the forces that influence their lives.

Cultural Models and Models for Teaching

In Chapter 3, I begin to detail a model of teaching and learning that
brings perspectives from the community sports setting into the setting
of school. It connects the development of "Speaking Rights" and "Reading Rites" in Chapter 2 to an exploration of culturally and individually
inscribed "Writing Differences" and their significance to developing critical literacy. In order to conduct this teacher/research project, I arranged
to teach a section of college writing at the University of California in the
fall semesters of 1993 and of 1994. I configured each class so that the
majority of both males and females were scholarship athletes who in
many ways were underprepared in high school for the academic demands of college, especially in the area of writing. About half of the
students in these two classes were African American while the other
half was composed of Asian, Latino, and white students.

I designed this study to use both structured and adaptive language
and literacy practices like those revealed in the community sports setting and to incorporate a diversity of youth cultural interests and competencies to motivate literacy learning. This study shows how these students' writing voices and overall literacy development turned on an axis
of cultural identity and individualized representations that were intricately linked to their unique backgrounds, experiences, and interests.
This study was also predicated on my belief that underprepared stu-

dents could be greatly helped in their writing development through computer-mediated writing instruction. I had noticed the considerable competence and lack of anxiety in manipulating complex computer games demonstrated by the young players I had studied in the community sports setting. The most successful of these games offered a high degree of challenge and a sense of empowerment for the players. I reasoned that my students' writing would improve and that their learning to use computers would not be hindered by any lack of willingness to engage the technology.

Therefore, I established a theoretical framework for teaching and learning based on considerations of youth development in the community sports setting, a model that blended perspectives from Freire, Bakhtin, Vygotsky, Street, Ferdman, Gee, and Kochman. Additionally, I built on the work of Christina Haas (1995) and what she calls the "materiality of literacy." Essentially, she draws on the work of Vygotsky to help articulate the role of material tools like computers in the process of writing. She argues for a view of writing as a practice embodied in culture, in mind, and in the physical body and posits that writing and technology work in a symbiotic relationship. Her analysis clarifies how technologies are not just tools for individual use but are culturally constructed systems as well, manifesting the ideology and values of the society. Within this framework, Chapter 3 looks at ways that literacy development and writing specifically of underprepared students can be mediated through the use of computers.

In conjunction with a coaching model of teaching, I assumed the perspective of teacher as ethnographer, which I feel offers a transformative approach to teaching even when a teacher is not doing formal research. If students change dramatically, teachers need to have the perspective to engage students at whatever point they are in that change. As Lisa Delpit (1988) notes, "We must learn to be vulnerable enough to allow our world to turn upside down in order to allow the realities of others to edge themselves into our consciousness. In other words, we must become ethnographers in the true sense" (p. 297). In my study, this perspective also came to represent attempts to learn as much as possible about the students being served by simultaneously sourcing and challenging the various cultural models on which their experiences and perceptions were patterned.

Doing ethnographic research in classes, however, can involve more than adopting a particular researcher perspective. In an article entitled "Informing Critical Literacy with Ethnography," Gary Anderson and Patricia Irvine (1993) note that "ethnographers can select unique instances of a teaching method and submit them to intense scrutiny, thereby providing us with case study data of the processes and problems associated with various approaches to critical literacy" (p. 83). They further note that "[t]he intersection of language and power in school makes language and literacy contested terrains" (p. 83). My study of these underprepared college students and the cultural and academic contexts that often work to constrain their lives and learning helped to illuminate ways in which moving them toward literacy also moved them across ideologically contested terrain.

In Chapters 4 and 5, I extend the book's focus on transforming teaching and learning to high school English classrooms and to issues beyond literacy and writing development. Since the most fundamental and important functions of schools are achieved through communication, an important task of the two studies on which these chapters were based was to discover and describe patterns of communicative interactions in terms of how they affected learning in the classrooms. Courtney Cazden's *Classroom Discourse* (1988) provided additional tools that built on Hymes's earlier work for this kind of analysis in schools. Beyond being the principal vehicle for learning, classroom discourse carries cultural cargo as well. Consequently, the nature of classroom discourse is intricately linked to the whole of class culture, and it is revealed in the various ways that teachers and students construct the day-to-day reality of classroom life together. Chapters 4 and 5 look at both official and unofficial discourse in class to assess how the interests, attitudes, obligations, and rights of students and teachers are crystallized in these complex social systems.

Chapter 4 is based on a study of a public high school in the San Francisco Bay Area completed in 1995 which, among other things, featured a curricular intervention in one of the English classes that attempted to teach students to both critique and produce various kinds of texts stemming from African American youth culture and youth popular culture in conjunction with other more traditional texts found in school. This school was also going through the process of de-tracking all of its English classes in an attempt to change some of the institutionally structured differences among its various groups of students. The issues of tracking are especially charged because significant research has shown their detrimental consequences for certain populations of public school students, especially African American students who are disproportionally represented in low-ability groups and low-skilled vocational tracks (Oakes, 1985). So, Chapter 4 also examines aspects of this process as an attempt to change structural as well as interpersonal relationships in the school.

Chapter 5 is based on a study completed in 1993 of two English classrooms in a Chicago public high school. It assessed the pedagogy and curriculum already in existence in two of these classes. Specifically, my study looked at the instructional styles of two teachers of senior English. One teacher made a conscious and continuous effort to link literature to students' lived experiences while the other teacher initially did not. Like the study in Chapter 4, this study also revealed ways that popular youth culture as well as aspects of African American culture could be built upon in schools to motivate learning, including unique ways of learning some texts that are traditionally taught in American high schools. Students were able to use African American and youth cultural materials in personal identity quests as well as to better understand larger societal concerns. Essentially, students were able to probe issues in a variety of texts that attracted or intersected with their interests enough to sustain their investigation beyond merely superficial readings. In the process they were able to model some of the textual strategies to make more informed readings. The process allowed students, as one teacher aptly noted, "to really look within themselves and grow."

In Chapters 4 and 5, then, I continue to use the theoretical formulations of the researchers discussed earlier, which were helpful for understanding the sociocultural nature of language and the literacy practices in the community sports setting as well as in the college writing class. These formulations were useful for focusing on students' learning with respect to specific textual materials and with respect to the dynamic social, dialogic, and power relationships that exist between students and teachers, and among students. Studying these dynamics within these frameworks illuminated problems and possibilities for critical learning through the discourse and culture generated in these high school classrooms. The particular classes and school sites in Chapters 4 and 5 were also selected because they represented the high levels of ethnic and cultural diversity that is coming to characterize the United States. So, these two studies add to the investigation begun in Chapter 3 of ways for "Changing Classroom Discourse and Culture," both in terms of how the nature of urban classrooms is changing in response to difference, and also in terms of how educators themselves can effect change to accommodate difference.

Engaging the Play of Difference and Change

In *Playing in the Dark,* Toni Morrison analyzes how complexities of difference have been primarily posited in relationship to a white (usually male) conceptualized "first principle"—white supremacy—in language, literature, and life. First-principle intentions are often revealed in two broad strategies used to conceive of and control the play of difference—attempting to make it either invisible or oppositional. In oppositional mode, for example, blacks are seen as the opposite; the "other" of whites; nonwhites; or just as patronizingly, defective whites. These xenophobic reactions are also extended to other people of color, as well as to other groups that the society attempts to marginalize. Ultimately, both strategies hide rather than reveal the actual play of difference and work to make the requisite conditions for difference to defer.

Yet, there can be additional responses to difference beyond ongoing attempts to make it oppositional or invisible. This is partially seen in the current high visibility of certain aspects of African American culture. When picking up a newspaper or turning on the television or when strolling through a shopping mall, one undoubtedly sees ads like those from a foodstore chain in California saying, "Chill out at Andronico's"; or from Ben and Jerry's Ice Cream Company requiring candidates for their top position to write an essay under the title, "Yo! I'm your best CEO"; or from The Young Shakespeare Conservatory (endorsed by the *San Francisco Chronicle*), whose poster features a picture of Shakespeare "crossed up" in a rapper's pose over the words: "Meet the Grandaddy of Rap."

The extent that media, business, and even politics exploit the images, icons, music, and discourse of African American culture to contextualize and legitimize their ideas and messages is fascinating. The extent to which educators often filter these elements out of school settings is equally fascinating. In the grip of market forces, styles from black language and culture are used to sell everything from cars to cola. Admittedly, these kinds of responses often do not reflect substantive changes in power and perceptions. Merely repackaging difference for mass consumption as a commodity is not progress. But culture is complex, and in the cycle of transformations from cultural experience to commodified culture and back to individualized cultural experience, educators have to be able to sort out and value displays of cultural authenticity that are productive for learning and literacy.

Ultimately, it is just as important for educators to recognize and work against the differential opportunities and patterns of treatment predicated on race and ethnicity as well as on class and gender, which have been so extensively documented by recent research. New strategies for teaching and learning cannot be isolated from these central, enduring problems of inequality, which are all too often fostered in American schools and society. Beyond merely acknowledging cultural differences, schools must be able to incorporate multiple perspectives and practices that work and are valuable because they are reflective of diverse, colorful patterns that make up the fabric of American life.

Though underprepared or underachieving students are often central in the studies presented in this book, the purpose for looking at them was not only to find ways to bring them up to the levels of achieving groups. That perspective ignores basic problems with the content and structure of American education generally, which is failing to reach and challenge a generation of youth alienated from schooling at significant levels. This alienation is complicated, and perhaps facilitated, by the fact that as we move into the next century, significant demographic change is merged with a dizzying creation of new knowledge. By the year 2000, for example, Asians will increase by 22 percent, Hispanics by 21 percent, African Americans by 12 percent, and whites by 2 percent (Mehan, Hertweck, Combs, & Flynn, 1992). Also, by the year 2000, the knowledge base will expand exponentially with the impact of networked computers, significantly changing how information is used. In light of these possibilities, what new content areas will become imperative? What new intelligences and modes of learning will be needed to access them? What new skills will be required to filter and use pertinent information from the overwhelming quantities available in both disparate and integrated combinations of text, image, and sound?

Clearly, schools need to modify their focus on the mastery of content at a time when the possibility of content mastery is becoming obsolete. Reformed educational structures and processes will have to be immensely flexible to incorporate the changing cultural forms and products driven by changes in demographics, economics, technology and ultimately by changes in power and interpersonal relationships. These new structures must be able to reflect and facilitate improvisation and spontaneity while they encourage stylization and self-conscious expression. They must also find ways to continually subvert and extend perceived limits in a relentless pursuit of excellence—excellence that is defined in part by its relevance to the constituencies being served.

The impetus of diversity and change cannot be reconciled in the stances of E. D. Hirsch (1987), Harold Bloom (1987), and others who argue that schools should transmit a specific and highly immutable body of knowledge encapsulated in an authoritative set of books and references that they have defined as most representative of the American tradition. Mike Rose (1989) acknowledges this impulse in education as the seeking of "a certification of our national intelligence, indeed, our national virtue, in how diligently our children can display this central corpus of information." James Moffett (1992), on the other hand, suggests that rather than learning what a field has established, students must learn how practitioners in the field come by this knowledge. Instead of emphasizing the transmission of a specified body of information, the focus must shift to skills for accessing, valuing, and synthesizing increasingly equivocal information in conjunction with the critical skills needed for its interpretation and application.

New Century Schooling

In the last chapter I suggest what I believe are guideposts in a quest for a mutable curriculum and pedagogy for teaching it—mutable to meet the needs of the diverse student populations that comprise America's schools; mutable to encompass the fluid, rapid production of new knowledge with its increasingly transitory applications.

These guideposts reflect some of the challenges posed by African American and youth culture to our schools, which must change to meet those challenges.To meet the challenges, educators must examine ways that dialogical, receiver-centered language styles and adaptive literacy practices within a coaching/mentoring/modeling perspective in the community sports setting can inform strategies that effect change in classroom discourse, curriculum content, and class culture so that student voice and consciousness is enhanced through more critical and authentic learning and literacy development. They must examine principles and practices of teachers as ethnographers who source students' varying sociocultural backgrounds, experiences, and interests to better understand, use, expand, and blend the cultural models that pattern their perceptions. They must also recognize technological mediation of learning as embodied practices, which can either facilitate or constrain student development, depending on the pedagogical perspectives that determine how and what technology is used. Finally, educators must approach change from a perspective that teachers have agency to subvert socially constructed limits on human development by changing the very schools in which they work to better serve the lives and learning of students.

I present this model of teaching and learning in the form of a scenario of one classroom in one high school projected about a decade into the future. In connecting implications and findings from the other studies to particular features in the model I illustrate ways that a possible future is in process *now*. First, the subject areas themselves are significantly changed. For example, in place of four years of English, the school has a core requirement for fundamental literacy in language and communication(s). Students are given a foundation in American and world literatures, but the focus of their fundamental literacy in this area is on developing competency in and understanding of the issues and problems of language and communication including different forms and uses of language within varying sociocultural and political contexts. Five Fundamental Literacies: math and logic; science and technology; language and communication(s); culture and human development; and aesthetics and values are at the center of the school's curriculum and the content of these courses are continually revised by a school Faculty Curriculum Committee for each fundamental literacy. These five curriculum committees along with a Committee on Motivation, Instruction, and Assessment establish the intellectual direction and content of learning for the entire school. There are many other elective courses, but these five, year-long courses are required to be passed by all students. Students take one fundamental literacy core course in the second year, two in the third year, and two in the fourth year. Additionally, they are encouraged to take advantage of the year-long internship programs in government, businesses, health organizations, and community organizations. Inside these structural changes, however, the scenario gives a view of how teaching and learning can take place, thus extending principles and practices from studies in this book to a vision of new century schooling. It shows pedagogical strategies and curriculum projects operating to motivate students and help them develop fundamental skills to access, select, analyze, synthesize, and interpret information in a quest to understand themselves in relationship to others and how they all are dynamically positioned in social, political, and physical space. The key class in the scenario revolves around collaborative projects that culminate in performative, multimedia presentations that require active and integrative participation. It shows how the teacher's coaching, modeling, and motivation efforts provide springboards for the leaps of imagination in the students and how the project assignments allow elbow room for representation of the unique concerns and issues that flow from the variety of background experiences and interests of each student. In so doing, the students actively co-create the curriculum's content, and help make it relevant for understanding the circumstances of their lives. Classrooms and schools must ultimately be understood within the larger sociocultural, economic, and political context of society. The studies presented in this book also illustrate ways that teachers can have considerable agency to transform school discourse and culture by honoring and sourcing diverse cultural experiences and interests of students to bring about more critical learning. They show how some teachers are shooting for excellence in American schools by preparing students to effectively negotiate and constructively change the increasingly complex world they will inherit and inhabit.

Note

1. The *Cambridge Encyclopedia of Language* (cited in Pennycook, 1995, p. 36) notes the following:

> English is used as an official or semiofficial language in over sixty countries, and has a prominent place in a further twenty. It is either dominant or well-established in all six continents. It is the main language of books, newspapers, airports and air-traffic control, international business and academic conferences, pop music, and advertising. Over two-thirds of the world's scientists write in English. Three-quarters of the world's mail is written in English. Of all the information in the world's electronic retrieval systems, 80 percent is stored in English. English radio programmes are received by over 150 million in 120 countries.

2 Speaking Rights/Reading Rites: Language and Literacy Practices Outside of School

As it becomes increasingly clear that schools, particularly in the inner cities, are often unable to adequately engage and prepare many youth for the demands and challenges of the outside world, more attention is being given to the nature of after-school activities for youth. Based on its recent study of what students do during nonschool hours, for example, the Carnegie Council on Adolescent Development has strongly encouraged that special attention be given to the out-of-school experiences of youth by educational as well as governmental and business institutions.

Of note is the five-year study by Heath and McLaughlin of sixty organizations that involved approximately 24,000 youth (1987; 1993). They looked at how some neighborhood-based organizations created environments that facilitated youth socialization and development partially through providing opportunities for wide-ranging adaptive language uses along with specific methods of relationship building and programs that enhanced self-esteem. They also studied the governance structures, leadership, and histories of these organizations. As with schools, researchers found persistent dichotomies between the reality of the lives of the youth and the perceptions of that reality by the policy makers trying to serve them. They additionally found that over 90 percent of these organizations were located in communities that local city officials described as suffering from poverty, crime, ethnic tensions, broken families, and other related problems.

Interestingly, though local public officials believed that most neighborhood youth organizations had to be centered around ethnic interests, Heath and McLaughlin (1993) found that for the youth themselves, ethnicity often seemed to be more an assigned label rather than an indication of their real selves. Perhaps this finding is related to the notion that through the pervasiveness of electronic media and other popular cultural influences, contemporary youth may be increasingly aware of themselves as individuals and as part of a more global community of young people. This awareness could reflect the fact that some elements are consistent in the organization of youth culture, even as it remains fluidly embedded in larger cultural forms.

Along with other features, sports are significant in the organization of youth culture. Though this proposition is more associated with males than females, the African American community sports setting I studied in Chicago did offer a context for interactions between adults and youth which I believe also has intriguing implications for schooling of both males and females. I am aware that sports particularly are often used to reflect male-constrained categories of experience and perceptions, and black male involvement in sports is no less culpable in producing oppressive identities and behaviors. As Stuart Hall (1993) notes, "certain ways in which black men continue to live out their counter-identities as black masculinities and replay those fantasies of black masculinities in the theaters of popular culture are, when viewed from along other axes of difference, the very masculine identities that are oppressive to women" (p. 112). I will attempt to show how a directed focus on particular communicative and social development principles that I found to be at work in this setting are at varying levels applicable to situations of teaching and learning beyond just African American and male students. So, while acknowledging that there are significant gender considerations that this focus does not apprehend, my purpose in this chapter is to provide insight into the network of communicative and social relationships and the nature of the cultural contexts that shape them in this community sports setting. I believe that these community styles and practices provide one model of how certain competencies are produced, and their description sets a framework for beginning to connect the language and literacy development that occurred in this setting to issues of classroom discourse and learning in schools.

A number of researchers have emphasized the significance of athletic coaching relationships to youth social and language development (Braddock, 1980; Fine, 1979, 1987; Fine & Mechling, 1993; Heath, 1991; Heath & Langman, 1994; Mahiri, 1991). Until around the mid-eighties, studies on youth involvement in sports programs were characterized by descriptions of things such as the number of participants involved, their attitudes about involvement, and the frequency and types of injuries incurred. More recent studies, however, have looked directly for connections between sports and learning with a number of them focusing specifically on African American males (Anderson, 1990; Braddock et al., 1991; Dawkins, 1982; Harris & Hunt, 1982; Picou, 1978; Snyder & Spreitzer, 1990).

Metaphors are an intrinsic part of theory building, and in education the idea of "teacher as coach" offers a fundamental reorientation of the roles, relationships, and responsibilities for teachers and students. As partially set out in Chapter 1, this metaphor is central to the Coalition of

Essential Schools reform movement which evolved out of the work of Theodore Sizer (1984). While conducting the study presented in Chapter 5 of this book, the school in which the study took place was in the process of becoming a Coalition of Essential Schools site. I was impressed with the Coalition's reform principles and strategies; its critique of the limitations of schooling organized around a workplace model clearly echoes aspects of Freire's formulations in *Pedagogy of the Oppressed* of the nature and limitations of a "banking concept" of teaching (Freire, 1970).

Yet, as I have noted in Chapter 1, though Sizer addresses part of the dilemma of students positioned as "objects" in the educational process, he does not go as far as to reconceive them as "subjects" in the sense of Freire—subjects who develop the capacity through education to critique and change their social conditions. Also, in a crucial way, Sizer's central metaphor for school reform stops short of its logical implication and thereby ends up recapitulating a key condition of the very workplace metaphor it was designed to replace. Instead of teacher as "coach" and student as "player," Sizer extends the metaphor instead to student as "worker." He disavows connections between play and learning that are implicit in his coaching metaphor. Rather, he states, "We can play at learning, without retaining much save the temporary pleasure of play. . . . Real learning and real teaching require more . . . and sometimes [they are] not much fun at all" (p. 2). I understand Sizer's desire to not diminish the nature of learning; however, based on the research presented in this book, I suggest that the unity of this essential metaphor be restored so that we consider teacher as coach and student as player in the game of learning.

The coaching metaphor as a reform model in major societal institutions occurs at a time of increasing marginalization of African American males and others in these institutions. Within the confines of this devastating situation, many young African Americans at times express a loss of hope and absence of meaning that gives rise to what Cornel West (1993a) has termed "a nihilistic threat"—a numbing detachment and destructive disposition toward self and others. Jesse Jackson, who has been speaking at schools across the country to help African American teenagers understand and work to reduce violence, has pointed out that more lives are now lost annually to young blacks killing each other than to the total of all lynchings in the history of the country and that, presently, fratricide is more of a threat than genocide. The emptiness, frustration, and displaced anger that gets directed both inward and outward is one of the bleak consequences of failed potential. It comes through emphatically in the words of an African American male teenager who stated that before he found an outlet in one of the programs of a community-based organization, he was "a loaded pistol." Some of these programs offer insights into ways to help these young people make sense of their lives and to redirect their energy toward productive pursuits.

I will attempt to show how a close examination of the nature of communicative and social interactions that are effective in the actual coaching of these youths can also help clarify the nature of interactions needed to be effective with youths in settings beyond sports. Aside from recognizing that this directed focus can itself be problematic if it is enhanced at the expense of others—such as females and other ethnic groups—I am also aware that much of the discourse and behavior associated with coaching and sports is not usually considered to be productive for balanced personal development. For example, the impression many people have of coaches is consistent with the characterization and caricature depicted in a short essay by John Skow (1993). He noted that "by the '50s, football coaches all behaved like George C. Scott playing General George Patton, and basketball coaches were getting into the act too. . . . [W]e get pacing, towel throwing and screams of rage, and a lot of other naughtiness that two-year-olds get sent to bed for." The notion that children's social and language development can be positively influenced through interaction with coaches is similarly troubling. Coaches' talk for most people is exemplified in Pat Conroy's novel *The Prince of Tides* (1986). In that novel, the coach addresses his team as follows:

> Now a real hitter is a headhunter who puts his head in the chest of his opponents and ain't happy if his opponent is still breathing after the play. A real hitter doesn't know what fear is except when he sees it in the eyes of a ball carrier he's about to split in half. A real hitter loves pain, loves the screaming and the sweating and the brawling and the hatred of life down in the trenches. He likes to be at the spot where the blood flows and the teeth get kicked out. That's what this sport's about, men. It's war, pure and simply. (p. 384)

An accomplished athlete in several sports, who now has two teen-aged daughters, told me that at forty-three he was still angry and working to unlearn the destructive machismo inculcated in him by coaches. By contrast, however, I found that the coaches and volunteers of the community sports program were quite aware of the negative possibilities of sports involvement, and they consciously worked to create a program that attempted to prevent many of these detrimental consequences. As a result, many African American parents, especially single mothers, in conjunction with community volunteers, were able to take advantage of the exceptionally high interest generated by basketball to give the Youth Basketball Association program, the YBA, a unique role in augmenting activities at home and school.

Participant/Observation Research in the YBA

To conduct this study of the youth basketball program of this neighborhood-based organization on the South Side of Chicago, I volunteered as
an assistant coach with one of the teams of twelve players for each of
two successive seasons. After getting permission from the organization's
director and the parents of the players who ranged from ten to twelve
years old, I recorded language use (with a portable tape recorder inside
a pack around my waist) and kept extensive field notes and artifacts on
other activities occurring over a two-and-a-half year period. During this
period I taped meetings of the coaches' council and the parents' council,
and I taped discourse at the weekday team practices and the weekend
team games. I also went to many of the special events coordinated by
the coaches and/or parents for the players, and I interviewed most of
the players on the two different teams that I assisted, as well as many of
the individual coaches and parents. I focused on two areas intensively.
One was the communicative interactions of the players, coaches, parents, staff, and other volunteers. The other was the structured and spontaneous literacy practices of the players associated with their involvement in the YBA.

I soon found that communicative interactions with the players took
place primarily with the coaches (who with one exception were all men)
and between other players (who with one exception were all boys), while
many of the literacy practices were initiated by members of the parents'
council, consisting mainly of women. I divided the communicative interactions into those that took place either inside or outside the "coaching circle," which was a key communicative situation, and I divided the
literacy practices into those that were structured by the adults, on the
one hand, and those that were adaptive or spontaneous (on the part of
the players) on the other. I used formulations from Hymes (1974) and
Saville-Troike (1989) as initial frames for assessing the communicative
interactions, and formulations from Heath (1982) and Street (1984, 1993)
as frames for assessing the literacy practices.

Hymes (1974) suggests three units of analysis: The communicative
situation, the communicative event, and the communicative act. The
communicative situation is the context within which the communication occurs. One key communicative situation was the coaching circle.
However, the communicative event is the basic unit for descriptive purposes because it involves a unified set of components beginning with
the same general topic and purpose for communication. So, specific communicative events were assessed in the coaches' circle as well as in other
communicative situations. Within the communicative event, individual

and identifiable communicative acts occur. Yet, observed behaviors revealed in these categories are actually external indications of deeper sets of codes and rules for interaction that must also be discerned. When possible, I attempted to illuminate aspects of these deeper codes and rules for interaction to reveal aspects of the competencies of the interlocutors. An essential finding was that communicative interactions in this setting incorporated a wide range of youth options or "Speaking Rights" that were characterized by being dialogical and receiver-centered, expressive and assertive, playful and colorful, as well as spontaneous and performative.

Saville-Troike (1989) synthesizes and amplifies the rationale for doing ethnographies of communication. In the community sports setting, I attempted to explicate her notions of the possibility of extending understanding of the relationships of language and language acquisition "to social organization, role relationships, values, beliefs, and other shared patterns of knowledge and behavior which are transmitted from generation to generation in the process of socialization/enculturation" (p. 8).

Heath (1982) defines a literacy event as "any action sequence, involving one or more persons, in which the production and/or comprehension of print plays a role" (p. 92). This definition was useful for my focus on the variety of structured and spontaneous literacy activities that I observed in or associated with the YBA. The role of the players in these activities and events was often such that they were encouraged or required to exhibit and/or practice both literacy skills and literate behaviors. Heath (1987) defines literacy skills as "mechanistic linguistic abilities which focus on separating out and manipulating discrete elements of text, such as spelling, vocabulary, grammar, topic sentence, outlines, etc." (p. iv), whereas literate behaviors were defined as abilities "to analyze, discuss, interpret, and create extended chunks of language-types of discourse that lie at the heart of academic study" (p. iv). So, in the same way that the communicative situation was assessed with respect to its composite communicative events and communicative acts, literacy events were assessed in part with respect to their reflection of literacy skills and literate behaviors.

Finally, in line with the work of Street (1984, 1993) and other researchers like Scribner and Cole (1981) as well as Heath (1983), I assessed ways that the specific functions of literacy in the community sports setting are embedded in larger social practices and reflect the sociocultural nature of literacy learning. The importance of this larger framework is clearly expressed by Street (1993) in *Cross-Cultural Approaches to Literacy*. Beyond Heath's definition of a literacy event, he employs "'literacy practices' as a broader concept, pitched at a higher level of abstractions and referring to both behavior and conceptualisations related to the use of reading and/or writing. 'Literacy practices' incorporate not only 'literacy events', as empirical occasions to which literacy is integral, but also 'folk models' of those events and the ideological preconceptions that underpin them" (pp. 12–13). Some of the novel forms of literacy offer additional understandings about the variegated nature of literacy texts and contexts as revealed in what I have termed the "Reading Rites" of youth in the community sports setting. Both "Speaking Rights" and "Reading Rites" are intricately tied to specific ways of coaching and mentoring these youth.

Mentoring Youth Development

The adult influences on this sports program came principally from two sectors—community volunteers and adults from some of the players' homes. As noted earlier, women volunteers worked predominantly through the parents' council of the program, while men volunteers worked predominantly through the coaches' council. Marvin Carter, for example, had been a volunteer coach for nine years before becoming the youth basketball program director. He was the only person directly employed by the organization to coordinate this program, which served more than 200 young people with three separate leagues and which practiced or played league games six days of the week for the seven-month season. So, the viability and very existence of the program was predicated upon wide-ranging support from volunteers. The role of the parents' council president, Amy Chandler, also reflected the personal contributions of the people who took responsibility for making the YBA work. Ms. Chandler had been a member of the parents' council for eleven years. She was also a math teacher at one of the public elementary schools in Chicago. She first became involved with the YBA when her son was a player. Even when her son had gotten older and was no longer in the program, she continued to assume significant responsibilities for coordinating YBA activities.

I will first look at the role of the coaches in conjunction with the players' language and social development, and then turn to the role of the parents' council relative to the players' literacy and social development. Ultimately, I will argue that the coaching circle as well as the structured literacy activities of the parents' council operated as a kind of zone of proximal development in which young players appropriated and practiced dialogical forms of discourse and aspects of critical thinking through interactions with adult coaches and other volunteers as well as their peers.

These coaches and parents' council members had never heard of Vygotsky or Bakhtin, but their goals for youth development were not without conscious design. For example, each new volunteer coach, as well as coaches from previous seasons, had to attend five mandatory two-hour training sessions at the beginning of a new season before being assigned a team. The mandatory training sessions and other meetings throughout the season revealed how the program director along with several coaches who had long-term commitments to the program were consciously attempting to create structures and influences to help the youths develop critical awareness, self-esteem, and values along with specific competencies and skills. The meetings themselves were designed to facilitate the coaches reaching consensus through dialogue on these goals.

The coaching philosophy centered on the value and practice of mentoring and the recognition that the most powerful influence on a young person could come from a meaningful relationship with an adult. To the person, coaches talked individually about mentoring experiences they had had while growing up, how the experiences were transformative in their lives, and how the mentor was usually, though not always, an athletic coach. The importance of young boys having men to talk to and model themselves on, and the personal characteristics of a good coach were more central to the discussions than specific game strategies of coaching. In other discussions these coaches explored how the transformation from being mentored to being a mentor harked back to earlier socialization processes in Africa between men and boys, with their attendant concepts of responsibility for others, values of sharing, respect for elders, and the development of competence and survival skills. They felt that a prime opportunity for bringing about these goals was in the communicative and behavioral frames of coaching.

I participated in these training sessions and found that I could not merely be an observer. In these meetings with other coaches and assistant coaches, I too reminisced about the men who had been key influences on me in addition to my own father, who was a good role model himself in many ways. But because of a distance that he thought should be maintained between children and adults and the way he positioned himself as an ultimate authority figure and disciplinarian in our family, I never felt comfortable talking with him about anything beyond the mundane.

I shared with the group some of my family experiences and found that most of the men in my age group with whom I discussed father/son relationships had similar memories. My father was a truck driver for a construction company, and once when I was fourteen he took me along "for company" on a trip from Chicago to Florida. We were virtually silent for the whole trip. The only redeeming memory of those endless hours on the road was of what I observed and learned about the vestiges of segregation that were increasingly overt the farther south we drove. Our limited communication extended into my adult life and has never been resolved. When I shared this experience, others in the group acknowledged that they, too, had felt emotionally distant from their fathers and had been unable to meaningfully communicate with them.

For me the void caused by the emotional distance from my father, was filled by two men, Rock and Mr. Wilson. Mr. Wilson lived three doors down the block, and when I was about seven he informally adopted me. He was married but had never had children; I had six siblings. He lavished attention on me, and I loved it. As in Wordsworth's poem, "The Excursion" (1814), where the speaker describes being befriended as a boy by an old man who "Singled me out . . . To be his chosen comrade," this sense of being chosen and of warranting the extended attention of an adult are engraved in my memories of childhood and adolescence. While sitting on the steps of Mr. Wilson's back porch or while helping him wash his Pontiac Bonneville in the alley, we talked about everything from cars to his experiences in World War II as a marine, to things going on in the neighborhood and in the world. I remember him telling me that his parents had never spanked him when he was growing up, and in light of my own experiences I almost could not believe it. The realization that children could be raised without being physically dominated or emotionally manipulated was one of Mr. Wilson's most important influences on me. Rock, on the other hand, appeared seemingly out of nowhere at the outdoor basketball court where I spent most of my adolescent summer days. He soon had our little group of ragtag players organized into a league with uniforms, refs, and coaches.

At the coaches' meetings I found that several other men had also had the same experience with Rock even though they had not known each other while growing up. Marvin was one of the men whom Rock had coached as a youth. After coordinating the coaches' meetings for several years, he was able to surmise that for more than twenty years and without any formal connection to a youth organization, Rock had been going all over the South Side of Chicago coaching and mentoring youths—a kind of modern, urban lone ranger.

During two seasons as an assistant coach—first to Carl Williams and later to LeRoy Crowe—I observed how coaches and other adult volunteers—like Rock and Mr. Wilson—shaped the structure of the youth basketball program through their influence and actions. Carl, for example, had been a volunteer coach for eleven years. Since his own son was an adult, Carl's long-term involvement did not serve a direct personal interest: his commitment was a broader social one, modeled on the actions of the man who had been his coach when he had been a youth. In one of the coaches' meetings, Carl talked at length about how this influence shaped his involvement. "I never had a father, but I did have a coach. So, I modeled myself on him. I know how important it is to have someone to model on as a young man. I think the coach should take [kids] off the court sometimes to do things with them. You are the representative of everything positive. He's going to listen to you when he won't listen to his own father, and you got to tell him what's the best school along with what's the best way to shoot a jump shot."

In *Sociology of Sport*, Harry Edwards (1973) notes that the role and responsibilities of coaches have been characterized historically as overlapping those of parents—particularly those of father. Carl and Marvin understood this situation as both a problem and a possibility, and over their years of working together they had systematized an approach to training each season's crop of coaches. Marvin was immediately responsible for this training. Using several written resources, he would lead prospective coaches through discussions to define and gain consensus on perspectives and strategies needed to achieve some of the goals for positive youth development in this setting. In one meeting that was typical of the initial discussions each season, Marvin spent considerable time trying to formulate what constituted good coaching in this program. He began by challenging each man to consider if he really could be a good coach "based on what we see as some of the characteristics of a coach: his ability to motivate, his ability to be concerned, feelings, caring, building self-esteem, building confidence, instilling discipline, instruct, teaching the concept of sharing. Be a good role model, somebody you can confide in." A prospective coach named Greg responded to Marvin by reflecting on a former coach of his who had those characteristics. "Even beyond basketball, I think we were, like, remembering that modeling. How he handled disputes with individuals, and how he carried himself as a man, and that was very important to me in terms of developing my own concepts and moving into manhood." Roger, who was also new that year, joined in. "It makes you want to reach your hand out to someone else because he stuck his hand out to me and a couple of my friends, you know. He believed in me to the point where I started believing in myself. And like now, anything I believe I can do, whether it's sports or out here in the work world, I can do it. It's like a positive thing." Marvin summed up their points. "That positive manner, we can, you know, get more benefits out of it. When I came up, you know, there was that re-spect for your elders. You listened to the adults or the older authority figures and you respected them. So we're trying to basically reestablish that concept through the structuring of these activities."

The mandatory training sessions and other meetings throughout the season revealed how the program director and several coaches who had long-term commitments to the program were consciously attempting to create structures and influences to help the youths develop self-esteem and values, as well as competence and skills. The meetings themselves were designed to help the coaches reach consensus through dialogue on these goals. The process involved affirming the adult coaches' experi-ences in being mentored as youths en route to confirming their commit-ment to mentoring youth in the sports program. This reciprocal process of going from mentee as a child to mentor as an adult coach was at the root of what made the coaching efforts viable for more than just athletic-skill development. It reflected the social motives of the coaches with respect to the overall development of the players.

Though the coaches tried to achieve consensus on a number of issues like the best coaching styles, effective team management, and contro-versial topics like what emphasis should be placed on winning versus having fun, there was variation from team to team and from year to year, depending on the unique personalities of individual coaches. De-spite the variations, however, there were specific coaching perspectives required of all coaches, and I saw two coaches removed because of vio-lations.

The efforts of the coaches' council were motivated by a pervasive belief that the youths in the program needed and could get much more from the basketball program than mere athletic skills. Gary Fine and Jay Mechling (1993), however, offer an important reminder "that the actual practices of children's lives arise out of a dynamic interaction between the formal organizations that adults design and the informal peer cul-ture that children bring to organizational settings" (p. 126). This com-munity sports program revealed insights into language use and devel-opment that occurred both in the formal discourse structures provided by the coaches, which often took place inside the coaching circle, as well as in informal situations of peer culture that surfaced in but were not limited to coaching circle talk.

Talk Inside the Coaching Circle

The coaching circle (or huddle) was a key communicative event used extensively by focal coaches before, during, and after both practice sessions and league games. During practices they were more relaxed with players, sometimes sitting in a circle for periods of time while the coaches discussed everything from set plays to game strategies, to skill development, to team problems, to administrative details of upcoming activities. During games they were more intense with players, usually standing or kneeling in a circle; yet the coaches' discussions would center on many of the same topics discussed at team practices. Despite differences in intensity, for purposes of talk between players and coaches, the two major situations for coaching circles had much in common.

Heath and Langman (1994) looked at the language use of coaches specifically and assessed a number of linguistic features that distinguished it as a register. I focused on the language use of both players and coaches in dialogic interactions. I audiotaped thousands of turns of talk and coded them as didactic, praise, criticism, conflict, persuasion, analysis, signifying, boasting, joking, and stories. I also assessed some of these language uses by the players outside of the coaching circles and in situations outside of the sports program itself.

Didactic with a Difference

Approximately 50 percent of the talk in the coaches' circle was didactic, with the coaches lecturing to players much like teachers often lecture students. Heath and Langman (1994) note, however, that although coaching is instructional it calls for organizational structures and language uses that differ from those of teaching, and they found numerous features that have not been found in instructional registers. I also found a number of instances where the style or function of these lectures were quite different from teacher lectures even though some features were the same. For example, at the end of approximately fifteen minutes of talk by coach Carl during the first practice session of a new season, he cued the players for a basic, performative call-and-response format. He started by saying, "We'll learn how to lose, but we'll also learn how to win. So look, we look like a good group here. The key to success and winning is what?" And, the players responded in unison, "Respect for one another." Carl reiterated, "So what will we always have for each other?" The players again responded, "Respect for one another." Carl continued, "Now when I talk you have to do what?" "Listen." "Do what?" "Listen!" When Carl concluded by saying, "What's the word?" The players responded, "Brotherhood!" "What are we about?" "Brotherhood!"

At that point in the season this bit of structured discourse contained three response concepts: respect, listening, and brotherhood. As the season progressed, a few others were added. The players clearly enjoyed these segments of mildly ritualized talk which, of course, were rooted in black language styles, and Carl was able to achieve a variety of functions through this simple language ritual. In addition to group bonding and getting the group's attention, it also functioned as a discipline device. When things were getting chaotic, coach Carl would sometimes yell out "What's the word?" two or three times. By the third time the chaos would be transformed into the unified response "Brotherhood!" Though these ritual forms for talk at first appeared constraining, they actually provided a simple, accessible structure for initiating talk and learning that later became more spontaneous and elaborated.

Praise/Criticism Links

The next most frequent use of talk in this sports setting was for praise. The players were continually being praised and reinforced by the coaches, and they also continually praised and encouraged each other. As games progressed players on the bench (an extension of the coaching circle) joined the coaches in a running commentary. "Almost there, Kendall. You're in the right spot. You're in the right spot for a lay-up." [Kendall fakes, shoots and makes the lay-up.] "Yeah Kendall! Nice fake. Nice move."

As one technique for focusing on players' accomplishments and improvements, coaches gave extended turns of praise both to the team as a whole and to individual players one-on-one as when coach LeRoy pulled a player to the side after a game to say:

> You played a good game out there my man. You know that? People weren't recognizing what you were doing, but the coaches saw what you were doing. You were playin' that point guard position. You were looking down low. You hit Kendall with a nice pass down there. You remember that pass he scooped up? You weren't hitting your free throws. But, I mean, we recognized that you stayed under control, and that's what we tryin' to get in terms of that person on the point guard position.

Coaches did criticize the players, but their ways of doing it were also interesting. They often contextualized their criticisms with praise as in the following appraisal of a player's performance by coach LeRoy in a post-game coaching circle.

> Hey, Kendall was jammin' in the center. He was blocking shots. You got two blocks. But the only reason he got 'em was he was out of position. He got a running start tryin' to get in position and that's why he got those blocks.

While praising Kendall for getting the blocked shots, the coach also criticized him for not staying in his defensive position. The point about his getting a running start was a humorous way of acknowledging that he was not where he was supposed to be on the court.

The discourse structure also allowed for players to criticize other players, and interestingly to even criticize the coaches themselves. Sometimes this helped to solve team problems; sometimes it created them. Yet, it was accepted that everyone had a right to express opinions about team strategies, midgame decisions, and player performances; and the coaches' circles before, during, and after games and practices were forums for this expression. In one exchange, for example, Kamau offered a criticism of the coach's game strategy by telling Coach LeRoy that the team should have played a zone defense against a good team that they had just lost to, making the point that the opposing team was too big for them to try to play man-to-man. When LeRoy agreed that he might be right, Kamau continued with a tinge of humor. "I am right. You gettin' too senile to coach." LeRoy just laughed.

When players criticized each other, coaches would allow them to air their views, yet they would often attempt to give these criticisms a positive spin. Players, for example, would sometimes take issue with each other's performances in games as in the criticism by Kendall after Arman had left the coaching circle to go to the locker room. "That's why I said don't put Arman in the game at the end 'cause when he get angry, he just gonna throw it away." Coach LeRoy responded, "Well that's a problem that we have to work on, tryin' to get everybody to see when you get angry, you don't play your best."

In these instances players' views and voices were encouraged and valued, yet players were helped to see how to make suggestions and criticisms that were constructive and focused on things that could help the team as a whole rather than dwelling on personal differences.

Criticism/Conflict Links

The game and practice environments were extremely noisy, high-energy, and fast paced, and at times criticisms modulated into brief arguments, challenges, or confrontations known as conflict talk. There has not been a lot of research on conflict talk and conflict in talk, and Grimshaw (1990) suggests that studying it should improve our understanding of substantive areas such as child and adolescent socialization as well as race and ethnic relations. He noted "that dispute modes vary developmentally, by gender, by participant relations of affect and of power, and by the nature of the matter under dispute" (p. 3). What these dispute modes reveal has a lot to do with the status, rights, and obligations of the participants and reflects the nature of their relationships. They show, for example, who may or may not speak, when one may speak, and the rules for turn-taking, and how one may speak to someone of a different status.

In the youth basketball program, some disputes were serious while others were playful, yet both forms were marked by verbal and emotional intensity. These arguments had to do with things like a given player's quality of play, the way a player felt he was being treated in relation to other players, or disagreements about offensive or defensive strategies. Of interest was the way that coaches would often permit the players full expression of their anger or frustration, as the next exchange, which occurred immediately after a close loss by coach LeRoy's team, shows.

> *Coach LeRoy:* Hey, come here Arman [as Arman is walking away]. Come here Arman if you wanna play on this team.
>
> [Arman returns]
>
> *Coach LeRoy:* We told you that we had to give you these things [raffle tickets] at the end of the game.
>
> *Arman:* I'm not getting any raffle tickets.
>
> *Coach LeRoy:* You gonna get some raffle tickets. I don't know where you get this attitude from. You played more . . .
>
> *Arman:* I ain't goin', I ain't goin'[almost crying].
>
> *Coach LeRoy:* . . . time than anybody on our entire team.
>
> *Arman:* I'm not talking about that, man.
>
> *Coach LeRoy:* Well what are you uptight about?
>
> *Arman:* You gonna take Pheron out and put me in. Why didn't you play both of us at the same time?
>
> *Coach LeRoy:* Why should we play both of you all at the same time? Why you wanna be in all the time with Pheron?
>
> *Arman:* 'Cause I can't dribble the ball up the court all the time.
>
> *Coach LeRoy:* Then you can look around and try to pass it off to some of your men.
>
> *Arman:* Everybody is runnin' down already.

In this exchange Arman was on the verge of being out of control emotionally. The coach also was highly charged emotionally, yet he continued to let Arman express himself and thereby eventually get at the source of his anger. Ultimately, taking and selling the raffle tickets (a requirement for all the players) was not really the problem. Also, the coach's thought that maybe Arman was angry about not getting enough playing time was not the real problem. Finally, it became clear that Arman did not like playing the point-guard position when Pheron, the best player on the team, was not in the game because it put all the pressure on Arman to bring the ball up court by himself. Though the coach finally responded in a rather critical way, he did allow the player to express his perspective and frustration at the way the game had gone and thus was able to get closer to the root of the problem, which had nothing to do with the first issue of conflict—the selling of the raffle ticket.

Though this exchange initially appeared to be defiance of an adult by a child over the selling of raffle tickets, it actually was more about the player's perceived loss of status as a point-guard based on how he performed in the game. In contrast to most school settings where a conflictual conversation might have stalled on the initial issue of the child not doing exactly as he was told by an adult, the player in the community sports setting had more latitude to continue in communication with the adult until the true cause of discontent was revealed.

Additionally, because there were several adults involved with each team, players also benefited by the presence of different adult perspectives or found that they could perhaps communicate with one adult when they were having problems communicating with another. In some ways this communicative situation parallels having two parents in the home. Children in both settings have a social, emotional, and communicative cushion to fall back on when things are strained with one particular adult. In classrooms (and single-parent homes for that matter) this is generally not the case. Because there is only one person to confirm or negate, children may not always have the opportunity to express themselves or to develop their viewpoints.

Persuasion/Analysis Links

Players had to sell tickets for the various fundraising events created by the adult volunteers to provide more financial support to the sports program. Consequently, the players were often calling upon their relatives and neighbors to persuade them to buy raffle tickets or admission tickets for these events. Since players perceived this effort as a chore, they did it rather half-heartedly. But these situations are not indicative of their abilities to be persuasive. When motivated, players proved they could be highly persuasive. For example, when attempting to get more playing time, players often became their own advocates. Although there were strict rules to ensure that all the players were able to play for at least half the game, individual players would still try to persuade coaches to give them more playing time. The following appeal is a good example.

> *Pheron:* You need me in there coach. I can stop Jason [a good offensive player on the opposing team].
>
> *Coach LeRoy:* You just came out. I can't put you right back.
>
> *Pheron:* But that's why they put Jason back now, 'cause you took *me* out. They coach know I'll shut him down. He only go to his right.

Coach LeRoy: You just came out Pheron.

Pheron: You can play anybody you want in the last quarter. He runnin' over us. I held him down to two in the first half.

In this brief exchange, Pheron supports his claim with evidence from his performance in the first half, his knowledge of the rules of the league, his assessment of the opposing coach's strategy, and his analysis of Jason's weak point. Pheron provides the kind of evidence he thinks will influence the coach, yet his ability to do this comes in part from constantly hearing the coach give similar assessments in his coaches' circle talks to prepare his players for their games.

The way players took on and replicated some of the structures of coaches' talk is further revealed in a kind of talk that extended from the coaches' circle into the players' lives at home. While playing a computer sport video game called "Hoops," for example, a player named Kamau not only adopted coaching jargon, he also revealed coaching methods of analysis of the game in progress.

Kamau: He bashed my crap, like some baloney, Dag . . . I ain't charge him. . . . I should have had you face it and pass it. . . . Dag, they usin' all they forces. I need a good passer and a good defensive man. Dag, man they got a three-point lead over me. Yes! Got that chargin'. Nooo! He got my stuff. I cain't pass my stuff, but he can pass his . . . Uh, good shot! Uh, work the ball in there with some effective passin' baby. Bring the lead down to two. Nooo! [Hits the video screen] Uh, dunk it. Down to one. Come on baby, we can beat 'em. This is a rough game. We want the ball, that's all we want. Take it from him. No. No! He won! Ah! I gotta do that again. I got a new strategy now. I want a good all around player, a good pass maker . . . They got a cold team though.

The computer communicated to Kamau through audible words from the announcer, the players, the referees, and the coaches, as well as through printed material that appeared on the screen. There were also fans cheering and booing in the background. Kamau's dialogue had at least four foci. Since he completely controlled the actions of one key player on his team, sometimes he responded as if he were the player himself. In this persona Kamau was sometimes talking to himself as the player; "He bashed my crap, like some baloney Dag"; sometimes in dialogue with the referees in response to a call; "I ain't charge him"; and sometimes in communication with other players on the team; "Uh, good shot! . . . Uh, dunk it." When he communicated with other players on his team he sometimes switched to yet another persona, that of coach— "Uh, work the ball in there with some effective passin' baby. . . . Come on baby, we can beat 'em." In the persona of coach, Kamau not only adapted coaching jargon, he also revealed coaching methods of analysis of the game in progress, "I should have had you fake it and pass it. . . . I got a new strategy now. I want a good all around player, a good pass maker."

This discourse production while playing computer games can still be seen as a form of language use that facilitates the development of language competence. With computer sport games like "Hoops," preadolescents like Kamau were in dialogue with computer-generated texts that were both oral and written. The computer texts were flexible enough to allow for communicative interactions that were both spontaneous and at significant levels of abstraction, i.e., permitting shifting foci and the adoption of more than one persona. There were instances where Kamau challenged the computer text when it conflicted with his sense of adequacy or fairness based on his personal experiences with basketball as implied by his statement, "I cain't pass my stuff, but he [the opponent] can pass his."

These interactions with an oral and/or written text can be characterized by Dillon's notion (1985) of the youth "dialogizing on an equal footing with a text, going below the surface of a text . . . to confirm, revise, or reject its meaning as the . . . [youth] tests out links with his or her experience" (p. 91). Generally, the communicative interactions that were observed in this setting also reflected principles of receiver-centered discourse (as opposed to intention-centered discourse) that will later be discussed as one of the fundamental characteristics of black language styles revealed by these youths, both in and outside of the coaches' circle.

Talk Outside the Coaching Circle

There were numerous instances of player talk outside the communicative frame of the coaches' circle. In informal situations and peer interactions, players engaged in talk infused with instances of signifying, bragging and boasting, and stories and jokes. Abrahams (1989) noted that "Performing by *styling* is . . . one of the means of adapting oneself to the street world, of developing a persona" (p. 248). He further noted that "as a young man learns how to *style*, he is much more self-conscious of how he is coming over to the others, and he therefore constantly looks for openings in which he can demonstrate his styling abilities" (p. 249). Though these kinds of performances were initially viewed as specially marked ways of speaking to be understood within particular interpretive frames (Bauman & Sherzer, 1989), this perspective was later revised to see all speaking as performative (Bauman, 1992). In this community sports setting, players had numerous opportunities to develop and amplify their voices (and thereby actualize their emerging identities) in performative talk that also reflected a wide variety of black language styles.

Signifying

Researchers have defined the complexity of signifying in terms of both its content and its rhetorical structures. Abrahams' work (1976) concludes that signifying is a technique of indirect argument or persuasion. Kochman (1981) has suggested that "signifying in black usage generally means intending or implying more than one actually says" (p. 99). Mitchell-Kernan (1971) describes signifying as a pervasive mode of language use that is reflected in the language of black women as well as men and black children as well as adults. Numerous examples of signifying were observed in the language use of preadolescents during communicative events in or associated with the sports program. The conversation below is taken from a birthday party hosted by one of the coaches for his son Khari and invited members of his team.

> *Kelvin:* Awh, come on, just blow it out Khari.
> [Khari blows on candles]
> *Kelvin:* They all lightin' back up.
> *Dion:* Trick candles, trick candles.
> [Khari blows harder]
> *Kelvin:* Hey man, bad breath. [laughter]
> [Khari blows hard again]
> *Dion:* Spit on it. [laughter, several boys blow]
> *Kelvin:* Now, stop, stop, stop.
> *Drew:* They goin' out 'cause y'all breath stank! [much laughter]

Abrahams (1989) implies that the word "playing" as in "verbal playing" was roughly equivalent to "signifying" (p. 245). He also distinguishes "within the black speaking community, three basic kinds of street-talk events: those intended primarily to pass on information, those in which interpersonal manipulation or argumentation involving a display of wit is going on, and those in which play is the primary component of the interaction" (p. 246). The above language sample can be characterized as part of a communicative event in which play was the primary component of the interaction.

Of course, a birthday party is supposed to be fun, but these youths (whose language is consistent with norms of black verbal expression) recognized that whenever there was an audience, there was also an opportunity for the display and potential admiration of verbal wit. A key element in this signifying sequence is the way it was started. Khari, the boy for whom the party was given, had already been put in the "trick bag" so to speak by having to blow out the trick candles. In a communicative event where playing is the primary component of the interaction, one way a person can get signified upon is when a weakness or deficiency is displayed. Khari demonstrated a symbolic weakness in not being able to blow out the candles (even though everyone knows that they are trick candles). Yet, even this symbolic weakness invited a signifying comment and consequently the possibilities for additional displays of verbal wit.

Rather than being an indictment of weakness, the signifying structure defers judgment until a response is made by the person signified upon, thus giving that person a chance to employ his or her own verbal wit. This withholding of judgment and encouragement of verbal wit partially reflects a style of discourse characterized by being more "receiver-centered" rather than "intention-centered." Gumperz (1982) indicates that intention-centered discourse, reflected more in white styles, was characterized by conversational responses related to "what we think the speaker intends, rather than the literal meanings of the words used" (p. 1). Essentially, the receiver's responses are more controlled in intention-centered discourse while the receiver has more self-regulated options in receiver-centered discourse, i.e., the plan versus the play of language. In receiver-centered discourse structures, YBA youths were able to play with performative, assertive, and expressive language uses both with their peers and with the adult coaches.

Stories and Jokes

YBA youths often joked with each other and sometimes with the coaches and other adult volunteers. In addition to jokes, they also frequently engaged in quite a bit of bragging or boasting. Boasting is a source of humor characterized by exaggeration while bragging can be a serious form of self-aggrandizement. Communicative events in which youths were joking among themselves were structured very much like sessions of signifying or sounding, involving turn-taking and usually focusing on the perception or suggestion of various shortcomings. Yet they were different from signifying in that responses were often memorized, generalized, miniature jokes (cracking jokes) rather than spontaneous and specific (creating jokes). These youths engaged in verbal play, cracking jokes in a way that seemed to lay the groundwork for the same verbal dueling skills needed for signifying. Their jokes were also characterized by the fact that, unlike signifying, they were not directed at anyone in particular.

Occasionally they also told stories, generally funny stories, to each other and to adults, which in some ways resembled extended jokes. One relationship that telling stories had to telling jokes was that they were also recountings from memory rather than spontaneous discourse as in signifying or boasting. The motivation for telling stories, like that for telling jokes, was often that the teller felt he had something funny to tell. It was important, too, that adults in this setting—the coaches and other volunteers—took time to hear and respond to the player's stories. The following story was told to me while I was giving Pheron a ride home after practice. Before I could drop him off, I told him I would have to pick up my brother who was about a mile away smelt-fishing on Lake Michigan. This caused Pheron to recall a fish story that he told me as we drove to the lake.

> *Pheron:* I saw this movie, where a man and a woman are fishing. . . . The woman first is catching all the fish and the man is not catching anything. Then he gets a bite. He pulls and he pulls but he can't bring it in. The lady comes over to help him and they are pullin' and pullin'. The captain of the boat comes over to help and they all are pullin' and pullin'. Finally they get it in. It's a shark! Instead of catching a fish to eat they catch a fish that could eat them.
>
> *Jabari:* Uh huh.
>
> *Pheron:* That's like . . . what if someone was walking through Yellowstone Park or someplace and there were signs up sayin' it's illegal to feed the animals, and a bear catches you and takes a bite out of you. Then the forest ranger comes up and arrests you for feeding the animals. [We both laugh.]
>
> *Jabari:* I guess what the bear was doing was taking a bite outta' crime.

Pheron's fish story exhibited several discourse strategies that mark competence in oral language use. According to Gumperz (1982), "to create and sustain conversational involvement, we require knowledge and abilities which go considerably beyond the grammatical competence we need to decode short isolated messages" (p. 1). The first part of the story was similar to a joke in that it was a retelling of a remembered story from television that Pheron felt was humorous. Yet, the way the storytelling frame started—by using my earlier comment about fishing as a pretext to telling a story about fishing—related to Gumperz's point that "Conversationalists . . . rely on indirect inference which build on background assumptions about context, interactive goals and interpersonal relations" (p. 2). An interesting shift in the discourse occurred when Pheron amplified the conclusion of the television story to create his own story about getting eaten by animals. This process of amplification is fundamentally tied to language learning and learning in general. Moffett (1983) noted that one of the keys to learning is to be able to engage in abstracting at a conscious level. "The more one becomes conscious of his own abstracting, the more he understands that his information is relative and can be enlarged and modified. By perceiving, inferring, and interpreting differently, he enlarges his behavioral repertory" (p. 27). Pheron abstracted the irony of a person being eaten by a fish he caught from the TV story and transposed it with a slight twist into his own story about the irony of being bitten by a bear and then being arrested for feeding the animals.

The variety of ways that this community sports program offered opportunities for extended player-initiated discourse among peers and also with adults was impressive. The coaches and other adult volunteers provided qualitative conversational and behavioral interactions that framed the players' language and social development. The communicative events that occurred both inside and outside the coaches' circle were often dialogical, allowing flexibility in speaker roles. These flexible, performative, dialogical discourse structures were characterized by being receiver-centered while also being able to accommodate both spontaneity and convention. At times the discourse of these youths revealed significant levels of analysis or abstraction. Talk in this community sports setting was used for praise, persuasion, signifying, boasting, and telling stories and jokes. There were also instances of ritualized talk, conflict talk, and what I have termed computer talk. These communicative interactions encouraged and even required players to be verbally expressive while they allowed for or provided models for a wide range of discourse styles. Their potential significance for schooling will be explored later in this chapter.

The YBA and Literacy Development

In addition to their language practices, youth in the community sports program were engaged in significant literacy practices that can be connected to productive ways of thinking about literacy learning in schools. While communicative events were shaped by talk that occurred both inside and outside the coaches' circle, literacy events were structured into this sports context primarily by members of the parents' council, even though the coaches' council did promote literacy in a number of interesting ways. Also, the players engaged in an array of activities on their own that revealed highly sophisticated, spontaneous, and adaptive literacy practices tied to personal interests motivated by sports discourse. This was the kind of adaptive learning that Heath and

McLaughlin (1987) noted "comes most compellingly through direct need and experience rather than through moral or didactic precepts handed on from others" (p. 14).

Both the structured and adaptive literacy practices that occurred in this community sports setting offered insights into competencies predicated on youth experiences that should be built upon in schools. Yet, as Lunsford, Moglen, and Slevin noted in *The Right to Literacy* (1990), the natural curiosity and vitality of youth that causes adaptive learning is often stifled in schools, "rendering them silent, obedient, and passive and keeping them in their places" (p. 2). Lunsford et al. suggest more serious explorations of "literacies we do not see" to determine how these alternative varieties that exist in communities, schools, and workplaces are being supported or discouraged (p. 4).

The literacy practices surrounding the YBA program represent literacies that are often not seen—some of the alternative varieties that exist in communities. A further discussion of the goals and structure of the community sports program indicates ways these literacy practices were being encouraged and supported. Youths in this setting expressed a right to literacy through novel and sometimes elaborate literacy rites that were rites of passage into empowering realms of community and sports discourse.

Parents' Council Promotion of Literacy

The parents' council was primarily the province of women. Although any parent of a player in the program could be on the parents' council, it had about fifteen active members, and only two of these were men. The parents' council was not completely representative of the entire parent body. It was composed of a group of what I have termed "conscious volunteers" within the parent body.

The parents' council organized a number of activities throughout the season. Literacy events—defined earlier as "any action sequence, involving one or more persons, in which the production and/or comprehension of print plays a role" (Heath, 1982, p. 92)—were often incorporated into them. Also, the parents' council communication with the general parent body incorporated a continuous stream of literacy events for the players. Leaflets were the key way that the parents' council communicated with the players and their families. Because the players were on site at least twice a week for practices and games, they were the key contact points between the parents' council and the parents. They were encouraged to not merely convey announcements of upcoming events and activities to the parents, but to read the information themselves and both inform and remind parents of the times, places, dates, and the requested or expected roles for parents and/or players in the activities. The role of the players in these activities and events was such that they were encouraged or required to exhibit and/or practice both literacy skills and literate behaviors.

In addition to infusing literacy events into many of the program's activities, the parents' council also overtly reinforced and promoted literacy and schooling through specific actions. For example, in conjunction with the program director, they would often bring in sports heroes and other role models to inform and inspire the players and to reinforce the importance of doing well in school. In a variety of ways, a lot of attention was given throughout the season to the players' academic achievements in school. Honor roll students were given special recognition in several ways. For the second half of the season they had honor-student patches sewn onto their uniforms once players' grades had been validated. Additional awards were given to honor students by the parents' council at the end-of-the-year awards banquet, which included onstage visual and verbal recognition. Essentially, the character of adult participation in the program, especially that of the "conscious volunteers" was such that the energy and excitement young people brought to basketball were creatively channeled toward literacy.

Youth and Adaptive Literacy

Although literacy development was promoted extensively, actual literacy events initiated by adult volunteers correlated primarily with the mechanistic linguistic abilities that focus on manipulating discrete elements of a text that Heath (1987) defines as literacy skills. However, more sophisticated literacy practices were initiated by the players themselves. The literacy events that made up these practices reflected much more the higher-order literacy abilities "to analyze, discuss, interpret, and create extended chunks of language" (p. iv) that Heath defined as literate behavior. Spontaneous or adaptive readings of a variety of sports-related texts were the foundations of these widely occurring literacy events. Analysis of these kinds of literacy events revealed subtle codes and motivations for participation in peer group and community sports discourse. Several of these literacy events will be briefly addressed to illustrate the provocative ways that literacy was practiced in this setting.

Some of these literacy events in the YBA were structured around and thus reflected the NBA (National Basketball Association) and the NCAA (National Collegiate Athletic Association). Every team in the YBA league was named for one of the NBA teams, and like the professional and college teams, the YBA had a rather complicated league and playoff structure. In order to understand how their leagues and playoffs worked, players had to comprehend intricate diagrams and the written texts of other handouts they were given. But they went beyond comprehending these texts to demonstrating sophisticated analysis skills in transferring ideas between various written and oral texts. For example, the players frequently analyzed the characteristics of individual teams, compared the various teams to each other, and formed and debated hypotheses of which teams could beat other teams or which team would win the YBA tournament. These literate activities carried over to other texts as well such as the analyses of teams competing in tournaments of the NCAA, the NBA, and in the simulated basketball tournaments of computer games. In order to do these analyses they read significant amounts of rather complex print material in the form of newspaper articles and diagrams, basketball cards, and computer game booklets.

Reading Newspaper Sports

Each year, both major Chicago newspapers print diagrams outlining the pairings of the sixty-four teams in the National Collegiate Athletic Association's national basketball tournament. On other pages the sports writers provide about a paragraph of analysis on each of the teams. Additionally, there are full-length articles on several of the more dominant teams and players.

The youth in the YBA regularly challenged each other by trying to get the most number of correct picks for wins in the tournament. To arrive at their picks, they read and reread many of the analysis paragraphs by the sports writers in order to evaluate and compared the strengths and weaknesses of each of the teams, and they continually debated the validity of their various choices as the tournament progressed over a three-week period as they filled in their picks. These were intensive and extensive literacy practices during which players were highly motivated to analyze, synthesize, and evaluate significant quantities of written and visual material as a pre-text to their discussion and debate. It all took place outside of and relatively independent of school settings. A little later in the spring, these youth would engage in similar reading rites during the NBA tournament.

Collecting Basketball Cards

Other frequent literacy events surrounded the basketball (and other sports) card collections that many YBA players kept. I interviewed four YBA players about their card collections and was deeply impressed with the extent and sophistication of the literacy practices associated with collecting, trading, and selling cards. Players read successive editions of a publication, *Beckett's Basketball Monthly,* that assessed the value of cards, and two of these players had gotten their parents to take them to a card-trading convention. All four were quite informative when talking about the relative merits of almost every player in the NBA in terms of how valuable certain basketball cards would become. The amount of data that these children obtained and discussed was extensive. Just to stay abreast of the active players in the NBA in any given year entailed knowledge of twelve players on twenty-eight teams or 336 individual players in the league.

Considerable data were contained on each card. In addition to giving the birthdate, birthplace, height, weight, college attended, draft pick, and professional team of each NBA player, a card also gives four years of college career statistics in five categories and professional career statistics in nine categories for every year that the player has been in the NBA. Usually, there is also about a paragraph of narrative highlights in the player's career. All of the statistics, personalities, predictions, and endless considerations associated with college and professional basketball added up to a knowledge base (a discipline) that these youth had mastered to a higher degree than just about every adult they knew. As they sought out and consumed the various forms of written texts that had information they desired, they entwined these written texts with oral texts in spontaneous and adaptive literacy events. They extended their mastery by challenging each other orally and using either written texts or the outcomes of sports events for validation. In short, through their readings of newspaper accounts of sports events, basketball cards and guidebooks, and even computer sports game booklets and instructions, these youths had become authorities in a domain that for them had cultural value.

Playing Computer Sport Games

The players' experiences with computer sport games also revealed literate behaviors and literacy skills in conjunction with both oral and written texts. Their literacy practices within this framework reflected interesting ways of accessing and representing information and knowledge. Their motivation to play these games came in part from their interest in sports. But it was also linked to the fact that these games gave players a sense of both challenge and power. For example, one player on the team, Kamau, gave the following response:

> [T]here is always another level, a higher level to go to. Plus you get to play other people. And it might be in the control that you get. Did you read the book? You like, have you read the book all the way

through? . . . You control when the players go in . . . when they come
out. You control when they shoot, you know . . . when they pass the
ball, who gets to dribble . . . You control the team, you are the team.

Kamau kept referring to the booklet that explained the computer-
sport games, "TV Sports: Basketball" (1990) by Cinemaware. The booklet was twenty-four pages of single-spaced text with only four small
pictures that combined would not take up a complete page. He had de-
coded and applied the instructions in the booklet himself in order to set
up and play what appeared to be a very complex computer game. To
effectively play this game, Kamau had to analyze, synthesize, and evaluate a significant amount of data in order to structure his teams to give
him the highest probability of winning. The element of human competition, the opportunity to program and compose, and the realistic nature
of the game served as motivating factors for the players like Kamau to
apply literacy skills and literate behaviors at very high levels.

From Courts to Classrooms

There are certainly elements from the community sports setting that do
not have direct connections to teaching and learning in schools. Yet, the
principles for effective communication and behavioral interaction that
inform the community sports setting, as well as the insights that it provides into literary practices, suggest that there are many connections
that can be made between this setting and the school. In the concluding
section of this chapter, I will draw out potential connections between
the notion of teacher as coach and student as player in the game of learning, and I will link the essence of findings regarding speaking rights
and reading rites to potential transformations of classroom discourse
and learning.

Coaching perspectives and strategies have a number of attributes.
The more global qualities have to do with mentoring general youth development and modeling specific skills development. In their mentoring
and modeling, the coaches operated within zones of proximal development that Vygotsky (1986) has explicated theoretically, and they created
dynamic language and social interactions that facilitated the players'
appropriation and practice of more sophisticated levels of discourse and
thinking. The coaching circle and the structured activities of the parents' council created communicative situations and literacy events in
which language, literacy, and social development took place. The coaches'
and other conscious volunteers' attitudes and involvement with the players revealed how sincerely they connected with the players' lives and
learning, reaching well beyond the sports arena. The connections that

the coaches and volunteers made were first and foremost genuinely human connections, developed through relationship-building rituals and egalitarian attitudes toward the players, illustrating how strongly they valued and accepted the players as individuals.

Though teachers may not be able to be mentors to all of their students, the goals of mentoring to create caring relationships, to build self-esteem and confidence, and to open lines of interpersonal communication can be adopted as general codes for interacting with all students. To illustrate how this orientation could work in a classroom setting, explicit presentation of a coaching, mentoring, and modeling teaching approach—and its effects on classroom discourse and learning—is given in the next chapter, which focuses on underprepared students' struggle for cultural and academic voice.

Perhaps the most fundamental measure of the effectiveness of the modeling and mentoring activities of the coaches was the extent to which it was reflected in the accomplishments and improvements of the players. Teachers and school administrators are often assessed in ways that are not directly tied to actual student accomplishments and improvements. Being efficient with massive amounts of paperwork, running an "orderly" class, working on various school committees, and being well-liked by colleagues and supervisors can all contribute to a superior teacher rating in some schools even when students have not significantly improved. John Goodlad's classic study (1984) of over 1,000 classrooms and teachers, and over 17,000 students found that despite all the attempts at pedagogical reform, the main vehicle for teaching and learning was still the total group. It also found that not only was the teacher the pivotal figure in the group, but also the norms governing the group derived primarily from what was required to maintain the teacher's strategic role.

This orientation contributes to the dilemma of students being positioned as "objects" in the educational process—another set of variables to be managed. Objectification of students changes, however, when the classroom focus is centered on the specific needs, backgrounds, and participation styles of the students and when their actual accomplishments become the measures of efficacy. While it is true that ultimately students must learn to take responsibility for their own continuing development, implementing the principles of coaching would have the additional effect of positioning teachers and students on the same team with the same goals rather than, as sometimes is the case, situating them in opposition to each other.

Also central in the coaching perspective was the focus on praise. The importance and frequency of praise in this setting contrasts markedly with what goes on in schools. For example, Goodlad and his colleagues (1984) also found that only 2 percent of the classroom discourse in elementary schools involved praising students, a figure that dropped to 1 percent in high schools. Despite the fact that many studies have documented how positively students respond to sincere praise, students still perceive that the primary response they receive from teachers is criticism, the sense that they are being constantly judged and more often than not found wanting. Of interest on this point is the way coaches in the community sports setting offered an ameliorative approach to criticism by also linking it with praise. Much can be learned, too, from ways that adults in the community sports setting attempted to elicit equal participation from all players while accepting and tolerating diversity in learning and participation styles. Also important were the strategies they used to make aspects of learning enjoyable or even fun.

On this point also, Goodlad points out that the emotional tone of the classroom was flat and the curriculum sterile. The implication from the student's perspective was that American education was immensely boring. The students' pronouncement was that perhaps what schools teach them regarding what they will later face in the workplace is how to endure boredom without protest (Goodlad, 1984). Based on the excitement of learning revealed in the community sports setting even though competition played a role, it is important to go beyond Sizer's formulation of the coaching metaphor to include the idea of the game of learning.

One aspect of the study presented in Chapter 5 reflects the viability of game structures being incorporated into classroom activities. When learning was most fluid in the high school classes of this study, students responded (as in the basketball league) as team players. These curriculum-based game structures stimulated learning because the students were highly challenged and the learning was both active or performative. These structures also facilitated a variety of learning styles, and they were paradoxically flexible yet ordered. They were flexible enough to incorporate spontaneity and chance, yet they operated by specified rules which were acknowledged by all of the participants. Competition was sometimes present, but when it was competition between teams of students, it essentially motivated more sophisticated levels of collaboration within teams as well as camaraderie and appreciation for the work of other teams. Just as the coaches and other conscious volunteers in the community sports setting recognized the viability of game structures for achieving a variety of developmental goals with young African American players, properly designed learning games in school are shown to be vehicles for organized discovery.

Speaking Rights

A key finding regarding communicative interactions in this setting was that they allowed for a wide range of youth options that I have termed speaking rights. These interactions reflected a variety of language styles that were characterized by being dialogical and receiver-centered, expressive and assertive, playful and colorful, as well as spontaneous and performative. Features of these language styles influence the discourse of other youths besides African Americans. But in this setting, these communicative interactions also revealed stages of the players' development of unique and personal voices. This development of voice through the speaking rights of the players was akin to Bakhtin's notion (1986) of voice as the "speaking consciousness" of a person. The speaking consciousness in these players was facilitated in a number of ways in the community sports setting.

Bakhtin's work suggests that all discourse is dialogical in that it is always in dialogue socially and historically, and it is always multivocal. But with particular instances of situated discourse, there can be varying dialogical qualities. What characterized the discourse in the community sports setting was the flexibility of its structures and its possibilities for shifting speaker roles. Players were certainly able to play with language and ideas. But they were also frequently able to initiate, challenge, and confirm serious or provocative ideas in discourse structures where they were assessed and responded to by adult coaches and volunteers as well as other students. In effect, they were positioned and valued as actors in the discourse and social dynamic rather than merely as recipients of certain desired effects. They were positioned as agents to consciously participate critiquing and changing their social world. This active engagement in persuasive talk, signifying, storytelling, jokes, and even conflict talk helped the players gain control over their words, construct language, and practice its use to express their authentic ideas, feelings, and points of view.

In several high school and college classroom contexts, the studies presented in subsequent chapters illustrate in a number of ways how key principles of language and learning in the community sports setting offer productive ways for rethinking the structures and practices in schools. Dialogical, performative, receiver-centered discourse strategies are linked to more student-centered classroom discourse and learning in which students initiate significantly more talk (and writing) as they struggle for critical, cultural, and academic voices.

Reading Rites

Participation in much of the sports discourse generated by these youths depended on close and extensive readings of certain "required" texts—newspaper accounts of sports events, basketball card collections and associated guidebooks, and computer sport game texts and instruction books. They were shown to be on an equal footing in dialogue with these texts, while making links to their own experiences. If there was a continuum, its direction was often from written texts to participation in oral texts for these youths. So, in part, their rites of participation in an empowering realm of sports discourse were also reading rites. In essence, these youths' engagement in and associated reading about sports was stimulated in a prolific oral and written discourse context that incorporated their needs and styles into the process of their social and language development. In contrast, as several of the researchers cited early in this chapter have noted, the natural curiosity and adaptive learning inspired by personal interests and direct needs are often stifled in schools.

In *Postmodern Education* (1991), Aronowitz and Giroux suggest that central questions in education today have to do with relationships between power and knowledge, learning and empowerment, and authority and human dignity. In *Popular Culture: Schooling and Everyday Life* (1989), Giroux and Simon further note that "[e]ducators who refuse to acknowledge popular culture as a significant basis of knowledge often devalue students by refusing to work with the knowledge that students already have" (p. 3). These considerations have important implications for what counts as legitimate academic knowledge and what teaching styles, learning environments, and content areas best facilitate learners in acquiring knowledge.

Findings in this chapter have illustrated how African American males, who are usually seen as at-risk students, initiated and sustained frequent engagements with a variety of written texts when they were motivated by the content. The perspectives and strategies in the community sports setting contributed to inspiring these youth to shoot for excellence rather than merely becoming "loaded pistols." Of course, these findings must be considered in light of the specific age, gender, and ethnic group that was observed. But for purposes of literacy development, they suggest that a better link can be made between what schools hold as important and meaningful and what young people find to be meaningful in their daily lives. The next chapter makes that link by focusing on a classroom setting in which the authentic experiences and interests of students were harnessed to enhance their writing development. It illustrates how principles and practices that are viable in the community sports settings can come into play in schools to help students develop their unique personal voices in learning to write and in using writing to learn.

3 Writing Differences: Struggles for Cultural and Academic Voice

This chapter begins to detail the contours of a pedagogical model drawn from African American and youth discourse and culture that were partially delineated in some of the findings from the community sports setting. It is based on a two-year study of a college writing classroom in which students successfully clarified and amplified their distinctive voices in writing while they gained competence in significant forms of academic writing. Many of the students in this study were exceptional, scholarship athletes. Several were national-class athletes and had been recruited by division-one schools all over the country. Often, their skill in their sport correlated inversely to their preparedness for college.

I tried to capture this contrast in a six-minute video that I made about this study, which depicted the difference between the students' lives in sports and in class. From a scene of a student hunched over a keyboard (the key spacing way too small for hands that effortlessly palm basketballs), the video cuts to the same student slamming down a spectacular dunk on national television. "He lights up a team," the announcer screams ecstatically. "You won't find a better freshman player in the country." In the heady prowess of microsecond reflexes captured in slow-motion replays, in the delirious adulation of fans, these are the "lucky" few that boys like those in my community sports study wanted to become. Most of those boys will never fully appreciate the tragedy they may have been spared by not realizing their "Hoop Dreams."

This study was designed to build on both structured and adaptive language and literacy practices like those revealed in the community sports setting and also to incorporate diverse youth cultural interests and competencies that would facilitate their writing development. The community sports setting provided a context that encouraged verbal expressiveness by both allowing for and providing models of a wide range of discourse styles that were dialogical; they allowed for flexible speaker roles and were receiver-centered and performative. The communicative events and literacy events in this setting revealed intricate language competencies and the development of literacy skills that contributed to the players' emerging voices on and off the court.

Issues of voice—their accompanying complexities of identity, authentic expression, and equality are addressed in this and subsequent chapters. The studies that are the bases for these chapters reveal how students struggle with complex issues of representation as they seek out and try on different identities in their passage from youth to adulthood. Yet the systematic absence of representation or the calculated misrepresentation of youth as well as people of color often stifles their attempts to define and understand both their distinctiveness and their similarities. This problem is partially tied to ways that the texts used as primary sources of school knowledge often present selective views of social reality often affirming and reinforcing dominant social, economic, and power relationships within the society. These studies reveal how teachers in a variety of settings develop ways to understand, acknowledge, and incorporate the varied identities of their students that emerge from and are influenced by particular cultural models as defined by James Gee (1995) in Chapter 1.

Representation

In its most simple definition, representation is the act or process of portrayal or depiction. Elizabeth Ellsworth (1995) points out, however, that curricula and teaching practices themselves can be understood as acts of representation, that "[t]eachers and educational institutions interpret and structure meanings into curriculums, and they mediate and produce official school knowledge through language, stories, images, music, and other cultural products" (p. 100). Textbooks are the repositories that educators draw on to interpret and structure these meanings and are thereby the main sources of school knowledge. Yet studies of textbooks conducted by researchers like Christine Sleeter and Carl Grant (1991) indicated that in addition to presenting highly selective views of social reality, textbooks also give students the idea that knowledge is static rather than dynamic and encourage students to master isolated facts rather than to develop complex understandings of social reality. Despite challenges from civil rights, black liberation, women, student, union, gay, and antiwar movements in previous decades, contrived or Anglocentric representations continue to dominate educational and other societal institutions. The potential for building on diverse cultural and linguistic backgrounds, interests, and competencies to motivate learning, by and large, is not accessible if the cycle of teaching and learning remains locked in a literature loop of textbook and canonical text representations.

With an understanding that writing itself is fundamentally a process that requires skills in representation, skills in the production of abstract signs in a text that represent specific meanings in the world, I focused the study presented in this chapter on strategies to extend classroom learning to major areas of concern and interest for the students. In linking their writing tasks to investigations of topics and themes that were important to them and in affirming a notion of literacy as a struggle for voice (Banks, 1991), I examined how their development as writers was revealed in the emergence of their writing voices.

This study was also predicated on my belief that computer-mediated writing instruction could greatly benefit underprepared students. I had noticed the players in the community sports setting had demonstrated considerable competence and no anxiety in manipulating complex computer games in the community sports setting. The most successful of these games created both a high degree of challenge and a sense of empowerment for the players. I reasoned that the benefits for writing that could come from the use of computers would not be hindered by any lack of willingness of my students to engage the technology. Also, in admitting students to the class I made sure that each one already had at least minimal typing skills.

In their report, *Research in Writing: Past, Present, and Future* (1987), Sarah Freedman et al. noted the importance of studying both the cognitive and social influences of new technology on writing development, including how computers may reduce or increase the demands of writing and how students make use of available technologies. They also underscored the need to consider patterns of individual differences in composing. My study revealed several computer-mediated strategies that significantly facilitated the writing development of underprepared writers by helping them to identify and build on these very patterns of their individual differences. Aspects of these computer-based writing practices also yielded unique insights into the composing processes of students, which have been difficult to apprehend by researchers since the early attempts of scholars like Sondra Perl, Linda Flower, and John R. Hayes (Flower & Hayes, 1981; Perl, 1979). Also revealed were ways that the technology provided specific heuristics for writing development, which are not accessible in noncomputer-based approaches to teaching writing.

Generating ideas and text to adequately develop a topic is a problem for many students, especially those who are underprepared in their elementary and secondary schools. I initially titled this study "Micro-Voices" because I thought that would be an interesting way to characterize the kind of writing that can go on in microcomputer labs. Over the course of the study, however, this title also came to stand for the initial "tiny" voices that some students bring to college. For these students, whose voices had been muted for various reasons, a significant part of the challenge was to help them to locate, experiment with, learn to trust, and eventually amplify their voices through writing.

Class Configuration

In order to conduct this teacher/research project, I volunteered to teach a section of College Writing 1A at the University of California (UC) at Berkeley in the fall of 1993 and again in the fall of 1994. Both sections were taught entirely within one of the new microcomputer labs. In the first year, I coordinated with another professor to concurrently enroll my students in his Psychology 1 class and with the director of the Athletic Study Center and one of the coordinators of the Summer Bridge Program to create a writing class composed primarily of students who had not passed College Writing in Summer Bridge. In the second year, I did not link the class to Psychology 1, but it was still configured such that nine of the fourteen students were scholarship athletes at UC Berkeley, several of whom also had not passed College Writing while in the Summer Bridge Program. There were only three female students in this class, but two of them were also scholarship athletes. About half the students in both classes were African American while the other half reflected the typical diversity of UC Berkeley's general student population.

Teacher/Research Perspectives

I used an ethnographic perspective in the research and attempted to let key issues for consideration emerge during the course of each semester. More properly, my research was a micro-ethnography in line with arguments presented in *Controversies in Classroom Research* (Hammersley, 1986) that a distinction should be made between doing an actual ethnography as opposed to employing selected ethnographic methods. It was suggested that much of the study of face-to-face encounters in classroom and school settings that employ ethnographic techniques takes the form of micro-ethnography. Use of selected ethnographic techniques by teachers studying their own classes has also been called *action research*. In such research data on students are collected through observations and through recording classroom activity and discourse; included are a number of techniques for capturing the variety of ways that students are able to report or reveal their classroom experiences (Bassey, 1989). I was aware that my observer's perspective both influenced and intertwined with the classroom experiences that I observed, and I will attempt to make explicit my own governing gaze that consciously and unconsciously configured my perspectives of both the teaching and the research.

In many ways, having the classes in a microcomputer lab was ideal for participant-observation. I constructed a teacher-as-coach persona (in this case a writing coach) in conducting classroom activities. Yet I found that an important part of my work needed to take place out of class, where it was crucial to spend time designing a good balance between individual work on the computers, interactive computer activities, whole-group discussions on our readings, and one-on-one dialogues between the instructor and individual students as well as between collaborative student pairs. When I was successful designing instruction in this way, I found that my role in class was dramatically different from the way I had earlier taught writing classes for years in other university settings. Essentially, like a coach prepares intricate strategies for a game beforehand and then attempts to implement those strategies in practice sessions as well as the actual game, my preclass planning allowed me to be more free during the actual classes to coach the students on their immediate writing practices.

The class sessions that were three hours long would often take on the tone of an office with students working at different levels and often on different assigned projects because they had some control over the order and pace of their task completion. This officelike tone was aided by my providing the students with a detailed assignment sheet at the beginning of the first class of each week. These assignment sheets informed or reminded students of the writing priorities for the week, providing further background on the various assignments to supplement our oral discussions about them. Students would take a break or two during the three-hour period and even leave the building to get refreshments if they chose to. Though I dictated the time constraints on breaks, the students individually determined when and how they would break up their work. In this structure there were extended periods during class when I could either interact with individual students or observe them separately or as a whole. I usually kept a field-note page active on my computer up front and I would often type in observations as class took place.

I had several ideas and strategies for teaching writing that did not depend on computer mediation and that I thought would be effective in helping these students improve. Because of prior negative experiences or the lack of affirming experiences with writing, many of these students actually feared having to write. Early strategies had to do with helping them overcome their writing phobias. Beyond the fear was a general lack of motivation to write. For many students writing had never been a valued or functional part of their social practice. Motivational strategies that I will discuss shortly involved the personalizing of early writing tasks, building on lived experiences, incorporating some popular youth culture materials, and allowing students to make a significant contribution to the curriculum.

I also structured the class around key modes of writing, moving from narrative and descriptive to analytical and persuasive and eventually to research writing from sources. I thought it was important that students be provided with extensive models for their writing. This began with my providing them with model works based on some of the criteria mentioned above; the next stage was for students to provide each other with model works that they had individually selected; we ended by selecting some student writing to serve as models so that students could learn from each others' work. A final consideration is what I call getting them to write like crazy. I wanted them to write, revise, and read more than they ever had in their lives.

Because students wrote more than sixty pages of text apiece and saved each of multiple drafts of every assignment on disks along with all hard copies containing my comments or the comments of peer editors, I ended up with close to 2,000 pages of electronic and paper text for analysis. I also kept field notes on both the classroom experiences and the continual individual conferences that I had with students throughout the semesters. Additionally, since many of my students had tutors who were graduate students in the School of Education, I collected research papers that some of these graduate students did on their tutorial experiences. I also interviewed some of these tutors about their work with my students, which along with their papers and other written responses provided yet another lens for analysis of my students' writing development. Finally, the introductory statements to the mid-semester and end-of-semester portfolio projects provided extensive texts of my students' reflections on their own writing, while the narratives in their class evaluations provided additional reflections on how they felt about their writing as well as the course generally.

Edited Texts

One goal in this study was to explore ways to effectively build on students' lived experiences, but it is important to note the outcomes that my students and I were building towards. In an interview that appeared in *Language Arts,* Lisa Delpit (1991) briefly discusses the term "edited English." She notes, "I think of conventions as the characteristics associated with edited English (and I use "edited English" as opposed to "standard English" because I see the conventions as encompassing more than what is generally meant by standard English). Edited English gives one the opportunity to reach large groups of people" (p. 541).

Delpit's distinction between the terms "standard English" and "edited English" is valuable, and I believe it also offers the basis of a construct for talking about the conventions of certain kinds of writing that have been sanctioned by the culture of power, without insinuating that other kinds of writing and speaking are consequently substandard or improper. Through the works of researchers discussed in Chapter 1, particularly Vygotsky, Street, Gee, Ferdman, Heath, and Scribner and Cole, it is clear that the functions for literacy are embedded in social practices. As we acknowledge and honor the validity of ways that students may be comfortable speaking and writing in culturally specific contexts, we can also make explicit and accessible the conventions, strategies, and skills that attend to edited texts.

This idea of edited English offers more than a mere amelioration of a problematic term. Beyond the negative flip side connotations of standard English is a consideration of the static and restrictive nature of the term. It does not encompass the intense, dynamic, and often collaborative activity that is required to produce each piece of edited English writing. It also suggests a unitary standard when actually there are many varieties of edited English that often vary within the conventions and styles that they sanction. The conventions of writing that appear in *Fortune* magazine are quite distinct from conventions of writing that appear in *Vibe.*

Academia is sometimes the scene of a collision of conventions. This was seen, for example, in many of the university English Departments that began offering advanced degrees in composition and literacy studies almost two decades ago. The conventions of writing in the social science fields that graduate students were using to study writing and literacy processes were very different from the conventions of writing in the field of literature familiar to the English professors in the departments that were beginning to award this new type of doctorate in English. These differences went far deeper than just considerations of styles recommended by the Modern Languages Association or the American Psychological Association. I know a number of former graduate students as well as professors who have dramatic tales of their involvement in these convention collisions. Yet, it is through the intersection and interaction of different writing conventions that writing itself is transformed and that new conventions emerge. Electronic mail, for example, is a contemporary writing practice in which the conventions are still in the process of being established. In e-mail some writers pay much less attention to general rules for spelling, capitalization, sentence structure, paragraphing, coherence, etc., as this relatively new form and application for writing continues to seek an accepted set of conventions.

I wanted my students to be aware that each time they saw a piece of writing in print, that writing had gone through and was reflective of an editing process. I wanted them to understand and be able to see that there were variations in conventions, but that there was still a discernible set of conventions associated with each kind of writing. I emphasized that there were times when a writer did not invite an editing collaboration but that these writings, too, involved the solitary writer editing her work through revisions. Building on these notions, I tried to make them comfortable with the fact that critical responses to their writing by me, by their classroom peers, and by their graduate student tutors were essential parts of the writing/revising process and that this was a process that all writers went through to varying degrees whether they were submitting their work for publication or in response to an assignment in a college class. In both the absence and presence of external responses, they too had to develop the strategies, skills, and knowledge of some conventions in order to effectively respond to and revise their own writing.

My strategy for beginning that skill development was to use one hour of one class period early in each semester to discuss and provide examples for five or six key uses of commas after which I gave students a couple of exercises to complete on their own. Commas are the most frequently occurring form of punctuation, and the uses that I selected for discussion reflected the five or six principal differences in the ways commas are used. Underprepared students invariably are confused on these distinct rules for comma usage, yet I have found that like the claim in the commercial for new glasses, in principle at least, they could get them in about an hour. I started with the simplest of sentences and showed how each successive use of the comma in essence allowed the writer to build on and significantly expand the meanings of these simple predications. Next, I argued that these five or six rules also revealed key aspects of the ways that just about every other form of punctuation was used. I demonstrated how semicolons, parentheses, and dashes could be seen as variations on a specific comma rule that we had discussed.

Interestingly, in a conference with one of my Asian students, he mentioned that he felt even more attention should have been given to teaching rules of grammar. He said that he had assumed much more of the class time would be devoted to formal grammar instruction. My idea had been to give a basic concept of punctuation and then to have times for students to work collaboratively in addition to working individually with me. Thus each student would benefit from my comments on their papers and through our in- and out-of-class conferences on the specific problems in each of their essays. I pointed out to this student that his own writing had improved considerably through this method and that it was through our collaborations on specific pieces of writing rather than more generalized instruction in grammar that I had seen my students' writing skills developing. In their course evaluations, the students almost invariably noted that this approach had been very effective for them. It did offer a specific and fairly elegant technique and set of terms for talking about the structure and development of their writing on a sentence-by-sentence basis throughout the semesters. I considered it the most fundamental technology needed for them to effectively engage in the editing of their texts as well as the texts of other members of their class.

Writing Differences

In Chapter 1, I cited Gilroy (1993), Gates (1993), West (1990), and Hall (1993) to frame an argument for understanding how differences both *between* groups and *inside* groups are dynamically constructed and positioned within historical, political, and socioeconomic contexts. The work of these scholars suggests that in addition to seeing the continual dialogue between groups and their positioning, it is also important to not lose sight of the particular patterns of individual difference within the broader group cultural identities. In one model of effective teaching and learning, students identify and build on these very patterns of individual difference. For writing instruction this model incorporates motivational content along with specific pedagogical strategies that draw on a variety of student competencies to elicit authentic expression of their personal and cultural knowledge. An important goal, of course, is to extend their knowledge, competencies, and motivations beyond their immediate personal and cultural frames to a critique of the larger societal forces in operation.

James Banks (1993) provides a description of knowledge construction in an article on the canon debate in multicultural education that was quite useful to this formulation. He defines five conceptually distinct but highly interrelated types of knowledge to help educators identify perspectives and content that could be used to make school curricula multicultural. These five types of knowledge are as follows:

personal/cultural, popular, mainstream academic, transformative academic, and school knowledge. *Personal/cultural knowledge* includes "concepts, explanations, and interpretations that students derive from personal experiences in their homes, families, and community cultures." *Popular knowledge* includes "concepts [etc.] . . . that are institutionalized within the mass media and other institutions that are part of popular culture." *Mainstream academic knowledge* includes "concepts [etc.]. . . that constitute traditional Western-centric knowledge in history and the behavioral and social sciences." *Transformative academic knowledge* includes "concepts [etc.]. . . that challenge mainstream academic knowledge and expand and substantially revise established canons, paradigms, theories, explanations, and research methods." Finally, *school knowledge* includes "concepts [etc.]. . . that are presented in textbooks, teacher's guides, other media forms, and lectures by teachers" (pp. 4–14). Using this typology, my model for the teaching and learning of writing directly builds on the students' personal/cultural and popular knowledge as the basis for establishing curriculum content. My justification is that these sources can not only increase student motivation to initiate and sustain writing practices but they also inherently provide avenues (issues and perspectives) for understanding and critiquing the societal forces that contextualize student lives.   Banks also discusses the concept of positionality that has emerged out of feminist scholarship. He cites Tetreault's point that "Positionality means that important aspects of our identity, for example, our gender, our race, our class, our age . . . are markers of relational positions rather than essential qualities" (1993). The concept of positionality has been used to highlight the importance of identifying the positions and frames of reference that underlie a person's scholarly work as a part of the process of evaluating that work. For my model of writing development, however, I turned the concept of positionality in the direction of the student. This turn was consistent with a concept of teachers functioning as ethnographers in their attempts to understand the personal/cultural backgrounds of their students and complemented the concept of teachers functioning as coaches; in this way it was possible to develop their students' writing skills, by drawing on their backgrounds. In addition to cultural differences, students bring to the classroom a host of personal differences which should properly be seen as markers of their specific relational positions inside their various cultural groups. The self-identification that was embedded in these relational positions of my individual students was fundamental to their writing development.

In this study, it became clear over time that students found motivation and content for their writing in very different personal/cultural and popular cultural experience and knowledge bases. Yet, definite patterns emerged in the ways that individual students drew from their interests and experiences. As earlier noted, the majority of the students in each of the two classes were scholarship athletes. Though I recognized that their identity as athletes was a relational position, many of them perceived it as their essential quality. There was tension sometimes between these separate perceptions, but I first tried to understand the significance of their athletic identification both from their perspective and as an experience and knowledge base for their writing.

In some cases events that occurred during the progress of the class caused students to question their identification and representation as athletes only. For example, a couple of high-profile athletes in this writing class were already beginning to see their dreams unravel. Two of these students had been among the best high school football players in the state of California. They both had suffered career-threatening injuries that prevented them from playing at all during their freshman year of college. Since even those who remain healthy and continue to develop face the ultimate reality that there are only a few spaces available in professional sports after college, the chances for someone who has been injured are even fewer. As pervasive as black athletes seem to appear in sports, there are only about 1,250 black professional athletes in this country in all sports combined (*Ebony Man*, 1992, v. 3, p. 45).

The gaps in preparedness are all the more glaring at a major academic university where black athletes sometimes have to endure opposing fans heckling "Prop 48" or "SAT" to call attention to special conditions through which athletes are sometimes admitted. Their high school teachers in some cases contributed to their underpreparedness by either being somewhat in awe of these athletes themselves on the one hand, or by not having any real expectations for them on the other. One of my students told me that he really had liked English all through high school, but his teachers never required anything of him in class because they admired his athletic prowess too much.

Stereotypical attitudes about athletes can also be devastating for these students in other ways as revealed in the following excerpt from a November 1994 article in the *Daily Californian*, the school's campus newspaper:

> A woman called the *Daily Cal* . . . livid about a photo we ran in our second Game Day special issue. It shows [two of the students in my writing class] . . . sitting in a line on the bleachers at Memorial Stadium . . . holding up four fingers. Our caller, a school teacher, was certain the two frosh football players were flashing gang signs, and was concerned that her students would get the wrong message about gangs.

> Now [they]. . . are not Crips, or Bloods, or anything close. The four fingers stood for 1994, their recruiting class, and if they're members of any gang, it's the one that takes the field at Memorial every day for practice. (Jones, 1994)

Athletes were in the majority in both semesters of these College Writing classes, and exploring their situations gives a bit of texture to the kinds of personal interests and experiences that some of them began writing from. But athletes were not given any kind of preferential treatment in the class, though I would go at times to see them perform on the basketball and volleyball courts, on the football and baseball fields, or on the track and in the swimming pool. The potential, however, for building on writing differences lay in identifying and incorporating the variety of ways that students found motivation and content for their writing and in discovering over time the definite but distinct patterns in their writing processes which could be further developed.

Alvin, for example, was an Asian student who loved science, especially marine biology. In a revised version of one of his initial papers he wrote, "I first became interested in marine biology fifteen years ago when my uncle bought me a goldfish and a small fish bowl. Since then, I graduated to a sixty gallon coral reef aquarium at home. I borrowed books from the library about marine life, and the more I read about fish the more interested in them I became." Alvin became one of our cutting-edge technocrats in the class. He would come to class early or stay late in order to surf the Internet. I would pass his work area and see him studying an online video of a frog dissection for his research paper. He accessed every source for this paper with his computer. Toward the end of the semester, I interviewed Alvin and mentioned that I noticed how he had been able to get something about science into almost every one of his papers, and we joked about the fact that at one point I had challenged him to write an entire paper without any mention of science. He responded, "I just felt it was that much easier writing about topics that I had familiarity with. So sometimes, when I'm stuck, I just think about science, and I see some relationships between science and what I'm writing. So, I just try to draw out that connection and put that in my paper."

An interesting example of Alvin's point could be seen in the first paragraph of a persuasive paper he wrote about attempts to ban *The Color Purple* which he titled "Percent Yield."

> In chemistry we learn that reactions require a certain activation energy to start the process. Depending on the reaction, the energy required to start it could be either high or low, but once the system goes over the transition state with enough activation energy, the reaction will proceed relatively easily. Reading *The Color Purple* requires some energy to go over its initial hurdles, but after that, the

novel moves briskly to reveal why it was deserving of its coveted Pulitzer Prize. With a little effort, the reader can learn a lot from this book that will benefit him/her for a life. This is one of the reasons why *The Color Purple* should not be banned in Oakland's public schools.

Alvin's best paper for the course, entitled "Teaching to Learn" described how insights from an experience as a Science-in-Action Intern had helped him make a difficult transition in his own life. This paper was actually reprinted in the university's Student Learning Center newsletter, but Alvin's comments about writing this paper also revealed the connection between writing differences and writing development.

> Once, my aunt, whom you will encounter in my essay titled "Teaching to Learn," tried to make a point about how little the average person writes. She asked me how many times a day do I write, not in a formal setting, but just for the sake of writing. Other than doing my homework, I never wrote for fun. I don't even doodle or write grocery lists. I came to realize that the thing I have to do is to infuse writing into my life. Though, I used to dread written assignments, I now enjoy them more in this class because I am able to incorporate my love of science into my writing.

Like Alvin, other students revealed unique patterns of difference and interest linked to their lived experiences that could be fuel their writing. Sport experiences provided motivation for some, but others, including the athletes, revealed rich and diverse identity quests that went well beyond sports. Jerod, for example, had an intense interest in popular culture, with a specific emphasis on rap music and the issues that it addressed. Additionally, he was struggling to reconceive his life and goals after being in a terrible car accident.

For Sarah, it was the exploration of paradoxes of identity and culture embedded in her Asian American experience as well as the power and problems of language (English and Chinese)—of gaining access to both worlds. Throughout the semester, she experimented with metaphor as a structural device in her essays as well as a heuristic for idea generation. By the end of the semester, metaphor had become explicitly a part of her writing strategy and a discernible marker of her writing voice. This was clearly picked up by the external evaluator of Sarah's end-of-semester portfolio, who wrote, "You have strong, interesting ideas and a very powerful, engaging voice. You also use imagery and detail well. I enjoyed reading your essays."

For Amy, a distance runner, initial motivation and content for writing was tied to decoding her sense of self as a white woman from a small southern California town and to distinguishing that self from her strict (single parent) mother who raised her. Amy's experiences in nature settings were another important, generative source. She rigorously explored the themes of many class assignments through the lens of an emerging feminist consciousness. She brought this emerging perspective to all of our readings, and in response to issues and questions addressed in *The Color Purple,* wrote a five-page, in-class essay exam that provided the most insightful analysis in the entire class. With regard to her own writing, Amy wrote, "After writing many different types of essays, I became more comfortable with my writing style, and I also became more confident when writing for other classes."

The sophistication Amy had gained in her writing during the class was also reflected in the comments of the external evaluator of her end-of-class portfolio who wrote, "Your introduction prepares me to read mature, well-developed essays, and much to my pleasure, that is what the portfolio held. Your maturity is best illustrated by your ability to extend ideas beyond a simple or predictable level. I also noticed that each of your essays explores the strengths of a particular woman. Have you considered taking a course in Women's Studies? I also hope you will show 'My Mother, Myself' to your mother. What a gift that would be."

Denise, a sprinter from Mississippi, also configured her writing around experiences that were gender based, but she built on her perspective from experiences as an African American woman along with family considerations that were also important to her. Leticia, single, Latina mother, used family relationships with her son and her estranged relationship with her father as a catalyst for her early writing. Ron and Bradford continually used issues from African American culture to focus their writing with extensions into youth and popular culture. They both shared with Sarah a fascination for imagery; additionally, there was an element of surprise in Ron's writing and an element of humor in Bradford's. Gerald, a swimmer who was white, was fascinated with complex sentence structures and experimented with an unusual writing style. With Ron, Bradford, Sarah, Gerald, and Ray (whose essays will be used as models to illustrate some of my claims for writing development), my advice for revising their work was often for them to temper the imagery or attempts at complexity in their writing. But they first seemed to need the freedom to stretch out to the margins of a writing strategy or perspective before winding back to a better balance of elements of effective writing.

A sample of the diversity of people and perspectives present in these writing classes is revealed in these brief profiles of a few of the students. By their admission, they started out in college with tremendous fears about writing. They were unaware of the nature and potential power of their writing voices, and they were insecure about many of the basic writing skills. Some of the computer-based work of these students will be used to further show how their movement from fear and dread to levels of comfort and enjoyment with writing was linked to a coaching and collaborative editing approach that refocused skill development and text generation around viable content areas and explicit writing models.

Amplifying "Micro-Voices"

One of the most prevalent problems of underprepared writers is generating sufficient ideas and texts to adequately develop a topic in writing. In my students' early essays, it seemed that no matter what the topic or mode of writing, they were only able to generate about a page and a half of text. So, I did something that I thought I would never do in a writing class. I set a two-page minimum on all essay assignments. I tried to get students motivated through the fuzzy logic of a sports metaphor. There were students in the class who could run a 40-yard dash in 4.4 seconds, which is blazing speed. I challenged them to break the two-page barrier. Of course, this barrier was not problematic for a number of students, but for those who were truly underprepared, it represented a rather formidable obstacle.

I started getting papers that began more than a third of the way down on the first page. Margins got wider and wider. Typefaces began to change from Palatino to New York, a slightly larger style of type. I even received a couple of essays where the type size had been pumped up from twelve to fourteen points. I commended these students on their "creativity," but I became more adamant about the requirement that they break the two-page barrier. I will later discuss how the use of concrete models of writing helped students develop and extend their ideas, but there were times when it was a little baffling as to what else could be done to aid those students who were having real problems with text generation.

I tried to help my students develop an editor's eye for recognizing the points in their writing that required more contextualization, more amplification, more detail. They also needed more skill in spotting redundancy or discontinuity in their writing. If they could learn how to do this, they would not only break the two-page barrier, but their writing would also significantly gain in clarity and sophistication. Jerod and I were working with these problems in an essay he had written about the terrible car accident he had been in while home on break. His injuries were so serious that it had not been not clear if he would ever be able to play his sport again. Another car had run a red light and plowed into the car he was driving.

Jerod's essay on this topic had lightly probed the provocative theme of identity. He wrote about how this whole episode had forced him to come to terms with who he really was as a person beyond the bright lights and cameras and the roar of the crowds. But in his treatment of this theme with all of its possibilities for details and connections, Jerod was still having trouble fleshing out what could become an extremely powerful and illuminating essay. Another layer of irony was that several articles had been published about this episode in the sports pages of major newspapers that Jerod had read. But he was having trouble breaking the two-page barrier and finding the voice to tell his own dramatic story in writing. While working with Jerod on this piece of writing, I hit on an image that seemed to help students see one way of clicking into a text editor mode for their own work and the work of their peers. It was a heuristic made possible by the way the computers themselves operated, and which I shared with the entire class. I was explaining how Jerod could look at the slightly developed images or episodes in his paper like they were icons on the screen of his computer. Though each icon had limited surface meaning, when he clicked on that icon it would launch a program that was rich and dense with additional meanings and details. Each icon on the screen was a window into a world of larger, more complicated, more detailed meanings. I gave him examples of the way he could "click" on a particular image or episode in his paper and launch more of the detail, explore more of the connections, or establish more of the context that rested just below the surface of the existing text. This computer metaphor became a useful way for me to talk to students about specific areas of their papers that needed to be fleshed out and pumped up in order to avoid a state of "arrested development"— a term I reappropriated because it was also the name of a popular rap group that some of the students liked. The best example of how this worked to facilitate text generation in a particular paper will be discussed a little later in this chapter along with the viability of using explicit models of writing. However, additional insight into how students like Jerod struggled to appropriately contexualize the elemental ideas and episodes in their texts was provided by Tony Mirabelli, the graduate student who worked as a writing resource person with Jerod. Working with Jerod's essay on *The Color Purple*, Mirabelli noted that the most common problem he came across was an excessive use of "unbound" as opposed to "bound" pronouns. The nature of these unbound pronouns— of referring not to something in the text, but to something in the context of a discourse beyond the text—created a meaning gap between what the writer intended and what the text actually specified to a reader. As will be seen below, when Mirabelli was able to question Jerod about who or what these unbound pronouns specifically referred to, he was able to help Jerod see the need to close this meaning gap with added contextualization.

Mirabelli discussed his assessment of Jerod's writing process in a paper for a class, "Language Study for Educators." He revealed how through his dialogue with Jerod, he was able to reconstruct the various sources upon which ideas in the paper were based, but that considerable confusion existed in the text itself because it left out the specificity needed to fully understand Jerod's argument. The assignment that I had given was to write a persuasive essay for or against the banning of *The Color Purple* as a high school text. The sources for ideas for the paper came from the book itself, from an article by Alice Walker that challenged a small parent-initiative to ban the book in the Oakland Public Schools, and from a semiformal, in-class debate on these issues. In addition to other texts, Mirabelli cited the following sentence from Jerod's paper: "For this book to win prize after prize, someone had to know if it was appropriate for high school students." Mirabelli essentially argued that the pronoun "someone" was unbound and its referents thereby were undiscernible to the reader. The resulting meaning gap dissipated the effect of the point that Jerod was attempting to make.

Unbound pronouns represent one of the ways that underprepared writers short-circuit the process of text generation by not understanding how to or not seeing the need to fill in the meaning gaps that exist in their writing. Jerod actually knew the particular referents that were hidden behind his vague use of pronouns. Jerod had carried his team in the class debate, making point after point to support the team's proposition and using specific data from both of the written sources as well as the data that came out in the debate. In fact, I was quite surprised by his perceptiveness of the key issues in the debate and how articulate he was in presenting his points orally. The opposing team was overwhelmed by Jerod's team, and after a while I decided to enter the debate to make sure that some of the key points of the opposing side of the argument at least were aired. But Jerod and his team members took on my arguments with insightful rebuttals, and the debate ended up being one the most significant class events of the entire semester. Later, Jerod received an A- on the in-class essay exam for which students had to write for two hours on five questions that I provided.

The point is that Jerod had significant ideas about the issues and arguments surrounding *The Color Purple*. That those ideas were not able to surface with the same clarity and sophistication in his writing is a key challenge for writing instruction. His unbound pronouns represented one of the many masks that hide the real ideas that students may have and intend to express in their writing. The rest of this chapter explores strategies for writing instruction generally and writing with computers specifically, which provide students with the tools and skills to identify and circumvent obstacles to text generation and the development of voice.

Computer Tools

In the introduction to her portfolio, Denise wrote, "I've come to enjoy reading and writing, and I am determined to move to higher levels of sophistication. Most of all, I've learned to love my computer which, in my case, was almost impossible for me to do." Subtly and dramatically, computers change the way we write. For underprepared students these changes can lean more toward the dramatic. Computer tools like spell check and the thesaurus that other writers might not give much consideration to can give underprepared writers power with words that they have never had before. The fact that the product of their writing is always in typewritten form adds a dimension to the work for some writers. At the level of visual presentation, it equalizes the products of all the writers in the class, and it also brings their work closer in appearance to the published writing they read. When I was a high school teacher, I noticed that some of my less confident writers would make the words on their page so small that they were barely discernible. It was as if the smallness and insecurity that they may have felt in the face of writing tasks was visually replicating itself in the diminutive characters they placed on the page.

At the most basic level, spell check helped some of my students save face. It was the first time that some of them could hand in an essay and be relatively comfortable that all the words were at least spelled correctly. Of course, this did not solve "their/there" and "here/hear" problems, but it did actually improve students' abilities to spell by highlighting only the words each individual student misspelled. Often there was a consistent set of these words that varied from student to student but regularly turned up in most of the papers. Therefore, the continued, directed practice on the very words that they had a tendency to misspell helped them to target and correct some of their spelling problems. When I was an editor for a small literary magazine, I didn't always know how to spell a word correctly, but I could almost always tell when one was incorrectly spelled. Spell check gave my students a tool that worked better than my editorial skill by finding spelling problems and offering instant corrections.

When I first presented data from this study and used the video that I mentioned earlier, another researcher challenged the viability of basic computer tools like spell check and the thesaurus. He was responding to Leticia's comments on the tape of how she used the thesaurus tool specifically. Leticia had stated, "I'll know basically what I want to say, but I'll know the way I'm thinking isn't the best way to say it. . . . I have an idea, so . . . a lot of times, you know, it will focus me on exactly my ideas." She had earlier mentioned the general uses of finding synonyms, etc., and that was what the researcher was responding to. Yet, on the basis of this part of her statement, together with what I knew about the way Leticia wrote, I made the case that Leticia and some of the other students had found this tool to be useful in helping them to stay focused on their emerging ideas right at the point where their idea generation was becoming blocked. These obstacles to moving the text occur both at the level of ideas and at the level of the word-by-word construction of an idea, and for some students the thesaurus prompt helps with both levels.

Since most underprepared writers have limited vocabularies when they arrive in college, I also devised ways for them to use the computer to increase the words they knew, along with the proper use of theses words in written contexts. I never taught vocabulary explicitly, but I provided ways for their vocabulary development to continue to be reinforced as they worked on the computers. I also recognized that extensive reading was the best way to build vocabulary, and the first book we read together was Mike Rose's *Lives on the Boundary* (1989) which had lots of words throughout that challenged my students. As we began our discussions of the book, I asked them to select ten words each from anywhere in the book that they did not know and that they thought would be interesting words for all the students in the class to know. I had them define their ten words and identify each, relative to both the page number and where on the page it appeared. After they each sent their lists to me through the computer network, I combined and alphabetized the words and printed out a copy for each student so that we had 140 words that would continually come up as we completed our reading of the book.

The only formal exercise with vocabulary was actually a writing exercise. For each student I selected another word from *Lives* for which they had to find all the synonyms in the thesaurus. Next, each student had to write a paragraph using every synonym for the assigned word in a separate sentence. Again, I combined and printed out all the paragraphs without the names of the writers and asked each student to choose the one they liked best and to defend their choice. So, we had the individual words motivating writing that motivated discussion about writing. One interesting consequence was that all the paragraphs were necessarily coherent, forced by the fact that key words in each sentence were already synonyms of other words in the paragraph. For these students, coherence is a difficult feature to achieve in writing, and this technique, which was facilitated by the computer, allowed students to clearly see and discuss the features of coherence operating in their own writing. This exercise also forced each paragraph to be seven or more sentences long because of the number of synonyms associated with the words chosen. In the early stages of the class, being able to write longer, more coherent paragraphs was an achievement for some students. Below is an example of one of the thesaurus-based paragraphs:

> The **estranged** man looked back on all that he had done through his dislike for the king. As a result of his hatred, he was **disloyal** and, being of high rank, sold the secrets of the kingdom for a bountiful price. He was **unfriendly** to dedicated and righteous subjects but acted cool and **indifferent** whenever possible to avert suspicion. Yet, he was too **discontented** to merely wait for the destruction of the kingdom. He wanted to **disillusion** the citizens of the ruined kingdom and turn them against the king. But the king eventually discovered his **disaffection**. Now, he contemplates his abhorrence in the dark, rat infested dungeon of the kingdom. For he was arrested and then sentenced to there for life due to his treachery and treason.

I almost never lectured, but if I did, some students would take notes on the computer. This was useful at the level of word processing because students learned to type much faster than they could write in long hand. Jerod, however, took this skill a bit further when I had decided to lecture a bit to set a basis for understanding how the evolution of Celie's consciousness in the first hundred pages of *The Color Purple* could be seen as being tied to the various people who came to Mr._____'s house after she was forced to marry him. This was an interesting structural device in the novel, and from Nettie, to Mr. _____'s sisters Carrie and Kate, to Sophia, and especially through Shug, Celie's consciousness of herself as a woman and of the oppressiveness of her condition emerged. Jerod came up at the end of that class and showed me how he had sketched the essential relationships and events that I had lectured about, using the MacDraw feature on the computer. He had given himself a powerful visual representation of what I had said. It was impressive.

Since we were using the Daedalus program that linked each of the computers in the classroom together in a local area network, we had a number of features for teaching and learning, including options for interactive written discourse. We experimented with most of the tools such as Daedalus Invent, an invention heuristic designed to help students choose, explore, and focus topics for their essays. We also wrote "real time" class discussions using Daedalus InterChange. I exposed students to the various Daedalus tools to see which mediums they were both comfortable and productive working in, with varying results. For example, they loved having written, interactive discussions initially, and there were interesting egalitarian characteristics to these electronic discussions, but after the novelty wore off it became clear that they preferred to spend "real time" discussing topics orally rather than in writing. One interesting feature of the electronic discussions, however, was that they often started out with joking and signifying between the students before getting down to any of the assigned topics of discussion. The most productive aspect of the interactive writing sessions in class was the fact that on occasions when good discussions did take place, a written record of the discussion was available and could be printed for the students' future reference and consideration.

E-mail, on the other hand, was very useful to the class because it offered us convenient ways to communicate outside the classroom. Unlike the capabilities for interactive, written discourse in class that made students question why we were doing this instead of just talking to each other, e-mail gave us options that increased our communication with each other. During the in-class Daedalus InterChanges, one form of communication took the place of another form. Through this networking program students were able to see each others' writing on their individual screens and to respond in writing to each other in a kind of dialogue. E-mail added another method of communication to the others. A brief e-mail conversation between Leticia and me gave one of numerous examples of how concerns were addressed or questions could be answered to extend teaching and learning connections well beyond the classroom:

> Jabari, I have a question about The Color Purple assignment. I wanted to know if I could focus more on the censorship issue and also incorporate The Color Purple into that. I think I can make my paper stronger if I do talk about censorship. I will throw in aspects of The Color Purple to make my argument stronger.

> Hi Leticia: If I understand your request, you want to emphasize the general issue of censorship with The Color Purple as one example. At this point without further discussion from you on why this shift is valid, I think I would rather see you keep the focus on the banning of The Color Purple with the general issue of censorship backgrounding that discussion.

By giving an assignment that could only be handed in electronically, I encouraged all my students to open e-mail accounts early in the semester. Once everyone had an e-mail address, I was able to create a class reflector and communicate about the class to all of the students simultaneously, as well as offer the option for individual communication between myself and students and among the students. Having e-mail also allowed us to get on the Internet to get information from university library sources as well as World Wide Web sources. Some students had greater interest than others in the Internet and consequently did more with it. For purposes of the class, I wanted the students to be aware of Internet resources, but for the most part the technology that we used for writing development had more to do with the word processing capabilities of the computer.

Co-Creation of Curriculum

One of the first committees I worked on as a new faculty member was the Faculty Advisory Committee to the College Writing Program. Committee members were each asked to observe a couple of sections of College Writing courses to get a sense of the instruction that was taking place. The instructor in the first class that I observed was using active learning strategies and curriculum content that seemed to motivate and engage the students. But, from the moment I arrived in the other instructor's class, I could see that there were serious problems. I got to the class a little before the instructor, and students began immediately asking me if I was there to evaluate their instructor. I replied that I was there just to observe, being a new faculty member myself. Still, they wanted to tell me about problems they were having with the class, and three of them even offered to meet with me at a later date, which I declined. I did begin to wonder, though, what had so alienated these students. I didn't have to wait long to find out.

The visits were prearranged, and this instructor had given me eighty pages of text that I dutifully read—text that was related to the discussion for the designated class session. The readings were of interest to me, and the instructor clearly had intense interest in this content and was well prepared with lots of notes and questions for the lecture/discussion. But within the first twenty minutes of this class that was scheduled to go for an hour-and-a-half, it was clear that the students were not just unmotivated or bored, they were experiencing a kind of pain. It was obvious that at least some of the students had done the assigned readings. Yet, motivating discussion was like pulling teeth. The instructor invited me to join the discussion, and for a brief time the two of us had a lively interchange which I hoped was demonstrating to the students that there were important ideas that could be plumbed from the readings. It didn't work. The tiny, restless movements; the slouching postures; the averted glances that would only come to focus momentarily—on the clock; the nearly unbearable silences; these students just wanted class to be over.

By the luck of the draw, they could just as easily have been in the other instructor's class, and their experiences in learning to write would have been very different. Beyond the teaching strategy (and I know there are many occasions and forums where straight lecture or instructor-led discussion works superbly) these students were being totally alienated by the specific content being used to teach writing. Unfortunately, their disaffection with the content, and to some extent the method of teaching it, also lessened their opportunities to improve their writing skills. It seemed clear that an overemphasis on content was not a useful way to teach writing in this class.

I have found it useful to de-couple curriculum-content mastery and writing-skill development in order to see them independently before deciding how they may best work together. There are many viable strategies for determining the curriculum content for writing classes. But too often approaches to teaching writing require learning a particular content in conjunction with, or in extreme cases requisite to, the development of the writing skills. I believe that for purposes of writing development specifically, the role of the curriculum content is to serve the development of writing skills. I tried to guarantee that the curriculum content in this study effectively served the individualized writing development of my students through essentially two strategies. First, I incorporated ways to represent and build on the students' lived experiences, and second, I selected particular kinds of explicit models of writing. At times, both of these elements converged in individual items in the curriculum.

The books I selected for students to read were *Lives on the Boundary* (Rose, 1989), *Generation X* (Coupland, 1991), *The Joy Luck Club* (Tan, 1989), and *The Color Purple* (Walker, 1982). Students also had to select an additional book on their own to read, review, and present to the class. *Lives* was written from a perspective that all my students were able to identify with, especially its chapter-long treatment of themes: wanting to be average, entering the academic conversation, literate stirrings, and crossing boundaries. This book is widely used in college writing programs across the country for these reasons along with its engaging writing style. I especially like *Generation X* because it trumpets issues and themes from the next stage in life that college students are moving to. It is also provocative and funny and written in such a way that lots of short, targeted selections can be used to model writing themes and strategies.

The Joy Luck Club and *The Color Purple* by being culture- and gender-bound necessarily focus on dramatic issues of gender, race, class, culture, power, privilege, generational conflicts, etc. I also chose these books because they have both been made into movies that most of my students have probably seen, and I wanted to be able to compare and critique both mediums. We eventually came to agree that *reading* each of these books was in many ways a more rich, more enjoyable experience than having them depicted for us on screen. As Denise exclaimed in the introduction to her portfolio, "I loved reading *The Color Purple* and through our discussions saw how it was much better than the movie." Students came to the same conclusion about *The Joy Luck Club,* and I had observed this also in Ms. Cato's classes with *The Great Gatsby* (see Chapter 5). For students, the motivation to complete a particular book or to become deeply engaged with it is at times connected to their experiencing it in a popular cultural medium. Here, however, through their critiques and comparisons, students were able to see the distinct characteristics and the separate strengths or limitations of written texts versus audiovisual texts. In the case of *The Joy Luck Club,* the discussion in one class turned on the depictions of the dramatic Kweilin story that was told early in the book. The narrator's mother told of having to leave Kweilin to escape the Japanese and go to Chungking with all her valuables, including her two babies, loaded on a stolen wheelbarrow that had formerly been used to haul coal. The wrenching ending of this story—when the mother tells her daughter of how the road between Kweilin and Chungking became littered with objects of increasing value including, eventually, her two babies as she and other Chinese people who were running for their lives increasingly lost strength and hope—takes up less than a page-and-a-half in the book. My students saw how the movie version with all the histrionics of its extended treatment of this scene could not compare to the "slap you in your face ending," as Ron termed it, of the written version. The epiphany that the narrator experienced when her mother concluded the story by saying, "Your father is not my first husband. You are not those babies" is also the reader's epiphany in the same instant. We agreed that nothing in the movie was as powerful in its impact.

Beyond these formal texts, I used articles from current newsletters, newspapers and Bay Area weeklies like *The Guardian,* and popular culture magazines such as *Details* and *Vibe* to give background for discussion and writing topics or to extend our understanding of topics for class discussion such as homelessness. I consciously tried to balance a sense of structure with spontaneity both in the sources I offered for writing topics and content as well as in the models I selected for writing strategies and styles. There were many examples of how viable these approaches were for students. Discussing what motivated him to write "Teaching to Learn," Alvin noted how one of the readings helped him with the topic for his essay. "I came across the idea while reading Mike Rose's *Lives on the Boundary* in class. The book was about Rose's experiences as a student and later as a teacher of inner-city children. I associated with the feelings of inadequacy and joy that he felt in his early teaching."

Another student, Gerald, attempted to model his writing on one of the readings. We had read the introduction and the first chapter entitled "The Culture of Hip-Hop" of Mike Dyson's book *Reflecting Black* (1993), and Gerald had become fascinated with a stylistic device that Dyson had used. He tried to model it in the first paragraph of his essay describing an "odd-ball" character. Dyson (1993) writes about black culture as follows:

> The incalculable grief and titanic inhumanities of chattel slavery; the unsayable trauma brought on by the erosion of embryonic liberties after Reconstruction; the sometimes acoustic, sometimes muted pain borne in response to the chafing indignities imposed by Jim Crow law; the stunning affirmation of race and culture that accompanied the transformation of social relations in the civil rights movement; and the inviolable courage and unshakable hope that ripple from religious faith all form, in part, the content of common racial history and memory from which black culture is fashioned. (p.xvi)

Gerald began his essay "Masked Avenger" with a conscious attempt to replicate Dyson's complex stylistic device, an effort that was somewhat reminiscent of an exercise in generative grammar.

> Knee-high soccer socks (one bright orange, the other red-and-white-striped like Dr. Suess' hat); large Dr. Martin boots with gigantic red shoelaces; baggy shorts worn by every day wear and tear with boxer shorts hanging out above the waist; a colossal T-shirt saying "Wang the dyslexic guy say's 'Yuck Fou'"; unwashed, uncombed hair mostly bleach-blond from long hours in the chlorinated pool; all wrapped in a Super Mario Brothers cape; this was my friend and former waterpolo teammate, Trevor.

Though there were definitely times when I asked Gerald not to go overboard with a given stylistic device and to be careful not to sacrifice substance for style, I nonetheless saw that an important way for him to practice and extend his writing skills was to map on to models of writing that interested him even when they stretched the boundaries of style. Gerald's case also indicated how flexible and varied a writing curriculum needs to be in order to comprehend the variety of different ways that individual students can develop their writing.

In order to truly build on the students' lived experiences, however, I had to allow them to identify their own issues and interests and design ways to incorporate these into the curriculum. This called for a co-creation of curriculum where students were able to participate in the decision making and the construction of content for what and how they learned. Because of their prior educational experiences, students were often uncomfortable with being given decision-making roles in the class, and they usually had to be encouraged to take on this responsibility.

This was in part my rationale for starting out with a set of texts that I thought would connect with students' backgrounds and interests, although ultimately I could never be sure what would work best for a given set of students in a given class. But the perspective was one of having a curriculum that could constantly and, if necessary, instantaneously change to accommodate students' contributions and decisions as they became more and more comfortable as co-creators of their learning experiences. This is partially what I meant in earlier discussions about the need for a mutable curriculum and pedagogy for teaching. It begins with a structure, but that structure can and must change with each student's contributions to the class. The teacher/coach has to be able to make constant adjustments to the teaching game plan based on the variety of individual contributions students/players are encouraged to make to the class/team. I found that the best way to build on their lived experiences was to provide ways for students to identify, explore, and affirm the things that were important in their lives, and to provide many avenues and opportunities for those things to surface in the content of our classes and in the topics of our writing. Invariably, the students offered connections for writing and discussion that were as significant to their individual and collective interests and developmental needs as anything that I could plan for them. But their contributions had the added advantage of making them collaborators and investors in the teaching and learning processes taking place in their class.

In the next and final section of this chapter, I have used the development of a single piece of student writing to exemplify ways that our co-created curriculum operated through computer mediation to improve students' skills in clarifying and amplifying their writing voices.

"Stentorian Man"

When Ray handed in the first draft of his essay titled "Stentorian Man," at barely a page-and-a-half, it exemplified some of the problematic characteristics of writing by underprepared students that I have associated with the term *micro-voices*. However, as I watched this piece of writing develop through several drafts, I began to see that key components of my notions of a model of teaching and learning were being revealed in the texts of this essay and the writing processes that created them. These components included mutable and motivating curriculum content that builds on the lived experiences and competencies of students by empowering them as decision-makers and as contributors to the content and process of their learning in a coaching/collaborating pedagogical style, which in this case also incorporated computer technology in the development of writing skills.

"Stentorian Man" was written in response to an early assignment requiring the students to describe an "odd-ball" character. Gerald's "Masked Avenger" mentioned above had also been written in response to this assignment. Students were asked to think about a colorful character from their past or present lives and to write about that person's behavior in a particular activity or event that gave insight into why or how the person was such an odd-ball. They were also asked to show how their interaction with or perception of this person either significantly influenced them or revealed something essential or important about them personally.

We had read and discussed several writings that described odd-ball characters. When students started work on this assignment in the first phase of the class, the initial models had come from me, but as they progressed through drafts of the essays, they provided other models for discussion. I would ask them to bring in a piece of writing that they liked a lot, and I would copy it for all the students to read as homework. On assigned days various students would anchor a discussion on the particular reading that they had provided. This was one method of getting them to contribute to the content of the class.

So we had discussed Kaufman, an odd-ball comic described in an article I provided from *The Bay Guardian,* who "more than anyone else pushed the dada edge of the comedy envelope" (Rahlman, August 25, 1993, p. 24). We had read about Dag in *Generation X* who described himself as "a lesbian trapped inside a man's body" (Coupland, 1991). In class discussions students made connections with other odd-ball characters whom they knew or had read about, like Jack MacFarland in *Lives on the Boundary:* "his teeth were stained, he tucked his sorry tie in between the third and fourth buttons of his shirt, and his pants were chronically wrinkled," but he could "teach his heart out" (Rose, 1989, p. 32).

We also read and discussed an article in a Dorothy Day House newsletter about a homeless man named Theomigabo who challenged the writer of the article on naive perceptions about homeless people ("Our

Daily Work," 1993). In response to this discussion, a student brought in an article from a local newspaper, which reviewed Howard Schatz's book *Homeless: Portraits of Americans in Hard Times* (1993). We found out from the article that Schatz's "Homeless" photographs were being exhibited at the University Art Museum which was less than a ten-minute walk from our classroom. Most of these students were not from the Bay Area, and they were shocked by the number and condition of the homeless people they encountered daily. In that class we decided to spend one of the periods viewing the exhibition at the museum. The point is that there were a variety of avenues that brought information, ideas, and issues into our classes and, as I will demonstrate with "Stentorian Man," these diverse sites of reading, discussion, viewing, and activity offered content and constructs that surfaced in and to some extent motivated the students' writing.

One more piece needs to be put into place. A tiny, one-page article entitled "Staking Claim," which was brought in by a student, presented a provocative theme that touched a chord with all of my students. They were able to see echoes of this theme in almost every work that we read subsequently. This theme of discovering one's cultural roots and valuing them was powerfully connected to a core issue in my students' lives. Their emerging understanding of the ways that they individually related to this issue allowed them to see connections between the material of their own lives and the material we read by published authors during the course. Like published authors, my students began to see how their lives and experiences provided valuable raw material for unique and authentic expressions, but it needed to be mined and processed with the tools of writing.

When it comes to what worked well for students, I don't want to overemphasize any single piece of writing over others. Students contributed pieces from Zora Neale Hurston, Margaret Atwood, Malcolm X, Robert James Waller, and a host of other writers. However, attempts to employ elements of either the thematic concepts or the rhetorical strategies from "Staking Claim," could clearly be seen in at least one piece of writing by each of my students, and the clarity along with the essay's brevity are useful to this demonstration with "Stentorian Man."

"Staking Claim" was brought to class by Leticia who anchored our discussion to it. As I noted earlier, Leticia was a single mother whose family relationships with her son and her estranged relationship with her father were a catalyst for her early narrative/descriptive writing in the class. It was easy to see why this article was significant for her. It was about a woman's relationship with her father whose influence on her life was consciously negated or resisted until she understood that those reactions had more to do with her than with him. It was about her coming to value and thereby to claim her roots. This theme, along with the writing strategies used to reveal it, made a profound impression on my students. Alvin acknowledged how he "found inspiration" for one of his essays in "Staking Claim." "I liked the way the author spent the first part of the essay describing the scene and within the last two paragraphs brought the essay to a higher level by making her own analysis of the situation. I tried to incorporate this structuring of ideas into my essay."

New college students are at an age and in a situation that forces them to consider complex issues of identity and family/community connectedness, especially since they have often been distanced from their familiar support systems, and they must consequently determine how they will represent themselves in and to a larger, stranger world. As Leticia used family ties, Ray, like Bradford and Ron, continually used issues from African American culture to focus his writing. He also found significant motivation in aspects of youth and popular culture, particularly rap music. Ray also shared Sarah's fascination for employing lots of imagery. Discussing "Stentorian Man" in the introduction to his portfolio, Ray noted, "In this piece imagery is used to shape the tone. For example, I used the sun to forecast the mood. Sometimes the sun rays gently hold me as if I were the last child on earth, creating a tranquil state. Other times the sun, 'lighting everything around me in a holocaust of yellow, orange, and red' manifests a cruel and harsh disposition." Intense, often overly intense imagery was a feature of all of Ray's writing. Even when we decided as a class to correspond with individual students from a class in a local high school to give them and us real audiences for writing, Ray's letters incorporated lots of imagery. A couple of lines from the beginning of one illustrates this, along with the point above that students like Ray, who is a formidable presence physically, were struggling through the scary transition from youth to adulthood. "Dear Betty: As I look out the window, clouds hang in the gray sky, creating a pervasive gloomy and somber mood. The rain comes intermittently, reminding me of good ole days when I used to sleep beneath the fire place, warm and protected from the cruel forces of the outside world. However, as I grow older, shelter and my comfort seem to fade."

The personal narrative in the first page-and-a-half draft of "Stentorian Man" began in Ray's dorm room with his listening to a "Boyz to Men" compact disc, procrastinating about doing his assigned reading in *Lives on the Boundary*. Finally, he was able to tear himself away from the music and head over to Sproul Plaza on campus, a place he thought would be perfect to do some reading on a Sunday. His reading, however, was interrupted by the stentorian man, "one of the strangest people

. . . [he] had ever seen [whose wailing] piercing sounds [a nonsense song with no coherent words] disturbed the calm." Ray noted, upon closer consideration, that these screams could have been like a warrior's call that "could have been beautiful if it hadn't assaulted everyone." Ray closed with the note that he was both frustrated and fascinated by this mystic man.

My summary of Ray's first draft is almost half the length of the essay itself. Through collaborations with me and his peer editor in our class Ray discovered how to employ writing heuristics, which included building on strategies from model writings we had discussed. "Stentorian Man" grew to more than five typed pages before being edited to become a final draft of three-and-a-half pages. My comments at the end of his first draft were as follows: "You have a good start here. The stentorian man is definitely an odd-ball. First, do a quick revision in response to the suggestions I noted, then let's talk about how your essay can be amplified to better capture both the oddness of the character and your reaction to him."

In the first conference with Ray, I reminded him of the metaphor that I had come up with while working with Jerod and that I had subsequently discussed with the class on a couple of occasions as a heuristic device to help them develop the issues, images, and themes in their writing. Ray and I went over and identified the menu of points in his paper that could be imaginatively "clicked on" to open windows through which one would see more of the details and more of the writer's feelings and perceptions that were necessary to give depth and texture to what so far had been only a surface treatment of potentially provocative images and themes in this essay. In our discussion we agreed that the essay as originally written had a menu of three basic items: Ray's mood and objective to read on a Sunday morning, a change in that mood posed by an obstacle to his objective—the stentorian man, and Ray's realization that beyond his frustration he was also fascinated by this man. Disclosing the elemental structure of the essay helped Ray see the fundamental decision points for further development, and it also revealed that essentially this essay was more about Ray himself than the stentorian man—an important consideration for refocusing.

At the first of these three broad decision points, Ray used imagery "to shape the tone . . . . [He] used the sun to forecast the mood." Ray lived in one of the high-rise dorms just off campus, and after substantial revisions, his dorm room view of the San Francisco Bay was vividly incorporated into the opening scene of his essay to give tone and texture to his psychological state as he wrestled with his procrastination about his homework. After briefly acknowledging his struggle to not jump back in bed and go to sleep, he showed how the beauty of the day itself and his recognition of the grandeur of the world right outside his window helped make him want to go outside and find a place to do his reading.

> I threw back the curtains . . . [and] the grandeur of the bay area morning emerged as if my window framed a canvas of a picturesque landscape. Like an art critic, I peered deeply into his painting and was impressed by the amazing detail. The bay bridge was like a huge prehistoric beast with tiny speckled insects buzzing along its curved back. To the left, the loading cranes on the edge of the east bay looked like giant horses, motionless and hypnotized. To the right, the Trans-America building rose out of downtown San Francisco demanding respect for its magnitude and aesthetics. In the middle of the bay, Alcatraz stood or rather slumped like an old man, warped and decayed by the passage of time, dead and dark on the inside. Rising behind this remnant of another era, the old lady A. K. A. the Golden Gate Bridge in all of her prestige and glory stood guard over the bay, beckoning in hope and pride, and everything bowed to her beauty. As I looked even closer, I could see the birds in the distance and hear their gawking as they flew above the trees that blanketed Berkeley. I could almost taste the whip cream clouds floating by when I realized that the aroma of pizza from Fat Slice down on Telegraph had floated up to my room. Looking at the clock, I remembered that I had to read for college writing. So, with a dollar and a Fat Slice coupon in my pocket and *Lives on the Boundary* in hand, I left my room in search of a place to read.

Whereas the dorm room scene in the first draft had lightly touched on the procrastination theme through Ray's listening to the "Boyz to Men" compact disc rather than getting on with his homework, he discarded that strategy entirely in favor of a much more extensive description linked to his room-with-a-view. We eventually used the final draft of this essay as one of our models for writing, and in discussing his work Ray talked about how he had revised this scene to communicate more than his procrastination. He noted how his tone of awe at the beauty of the sights outside his window was also designed to establish a mood of dreamlike tranquility against which his eventual encounter with the stentorian man would collide.

Ray further noted how the computer metaphor that we had discussed worked to help him develop both content and structure. In writing this scene, he tried to imagine that his dorm window was like the screen of his computer with each feature out in the bay that he selected for description being a flat icon at first that he would click on in his imagination to see more of the detail behind the surface image. To describe this in computer terminology, Ray had treated the broad decision points like three program folders into which he could drag-and-drop a variety of application/ideas to create a menu of choices for launching more contextualization and detail in his writing.

Ray operated on the next decision point in his essay—his encounter with the stentorian man—in a similar way. It had come out in class discussions that he had conflicting feelings about the situation of homeless people in the Bay Area. He had written another essay on that topic, "Them," which chronicled his shock at seeing a fairly young man and his three children sitting on Telegraph Avenue begging for change and food. The stentorian man was also a beggar "dressed in a red sweat shirt, corduroy pants, and sneakers with an empty cup in his outstretched hand." But as his skeletal description became clothed with more detail through successive revisions, the force of his presence also took on added significance as the axis on which the key theme as well as the structure of the essay turned. Unlike draft one, which cloaked Ray's frustration in a guise, allowing him to believe that the stentorian man's vociferous screams were preventing him from reading *Lives on the Boundary,* the final draft honestly and painfully probed the intense feelings of disdain that Ray was experiencing in attempting to read a real life on the boundary.

> I began to see him as the devil . . . . Wailing at the top of his lungs, he used his voice as a threatening weapon, scaring many people away . . . . Although I was unsure on whether he was upset that no one proceeded to give him money, or he was demented, I hated him. This morning's serene painting was being slashed forever by this demon.

Ray's revised essay went on to reveal how he was simultaneously fascinated by an eerie presence. "Something deep and latent in me was attracted to his cacophony. His self-asserting and commanding tone entranced me like the painting did."

I noted earlier that Ray, like several other students in the class, often chose issues in African American culture on which to focus his writing. One of his contributions to the class curriculum, for example, on which he anchored the class discussion was a selection from *The Autobiography of Malcolm X.* He was passionate about these issues. In one class discussion on *The Color Purple,* Ray strongly disagreed when I suggested that the book revealed ways that the oppression of black women was every bit as intense as it was for black men, and that black men did at times engage in destructive behavior that was not always the consequence of racism. Ray expressed his view that black men were especially targeted by racism and white supremacy. It was a view that I have heard many times before. It came out quite graphically, for example, in a scene in the movie *Higher Learning* which was not out during the semester of our class, but later had caused quite a stir. I didn't relent in my position; Ray relentlessly pursued his. He couldn't contain himself in his seat. He stood up in our "talking circle" and paced back and forth occasionally as he made his points. For a moment he was the man—the stentorian man.

"Staking Claim" provided a model that influenced the writing of a number of students in the class. They were able to explicate and to some extent emulate its thematic content and strategies in their writing. Leticia used it to think and write through connections with her father and son; it helped Amy understand and write about connections to her mother and sister; Alvin appropriated its rhetorical strategies to make connections in his teaching and learning; and Ray used its themes to explore connections to community and self. At the third decision point in his essay, in contrast to the open ending of the initial draft, Ray shares the epiphany of staking claim.

Ray used successive drafts of this essay to probe the tensions of this third decision point, and he eventually saw that these tensions were enmeshed in his own identity quest. Something essential about the stentorian man represented something essential about Ray. When he was able to embrace this essential quality of himself that was represented in the other, he wrote, "my mind was able to break through his wall of sound and on the other side a landscape appeared. It was Africa." In breaking through this wall of sound, Ray was able to stake claim on this other landscape which counter-balanced his earlier description of the San Francisco Bay. When he came down from the lofty heights of his room-with-a-view, he was also able to see something of equal grandeur "reflecting black" in a single life on the streets. He wrote:

> I could see her majestic mountains that rose out of the rich soil, touching God. I could see her powerful waterfalls and life giving rivers, that surged like arteries, with cargo as precious as blood. I could see her ancient ruins, calculated and precise that told arcane tales of great civilizations. I could see the great animals on the plains of the savanna moving with agility, dignified and proud. Beyond his wall of sound, I could feel the sun cradling my body like I was his child, taste the rich snow on the mountains, hear the varied languages springing forth from diverse communities, smell the smorgasbord of delicious food, and intuitively I felt that I belonged.

In the elegance of its structure, in the vividness of its images, in the light it sheds on life and learning, "Stentorian Man" speaks, indeed, in a loud yet lucid voice. It was one product of a process of shooting for excellence. Operating on an initially limited theme, Ray was able to use a computer heuristic for invention, along with the models of writing that were being continually critiqued in the class to help motivate and facilitate the intense introspection, interrogation, and invention that led to the final piece. Ray noted in his portfolio how he saw his writing and his attitude towards writing change over the semester. He wrote:

> The ability to write is a skill that can be taught at the most basic level. But the ability to write well is an art, learned only through an environment of extreme practice and evaluation. College Writing 1A, deemed dummy English by some people, produces no dummies. I honestly believe that not passing the Subject A exam was the best thing that ever happened to me. For this class has gotten rid of my most prevalent fear—the fear to write. With the help of my teacher and peers, slowly I am learning to express my thoughts in a clear, concise yet detailed way.

"Stentorian Man" was one of the many pieces of writing produced in the two semesters of my College Writing course. These products taken together provided insights into the composing processes of writers, in this case writers who started out in college being underprepared. It especially revealed some of the patterns of individual difference in the ways students compose, as discussed in the section of this chapter on Writing Differences. Though prompts like the odd-ball character assignment forced students to consider issues of difference, analysis of all the drafts of a particular essay through all the techniques used to capture and contain as raw data aspects of the students' composing processes provided insights into how writers compose differently. It was possible to trace the way a particular prompt or model was used by a writer to generate text through a close evaluation and comparison of the successive drafts on a topic. The illustration with "Stentorian Man" revealed considerations that influenced a student's composing process through all of the drafts of his essay, but I only displayed and compared actual texts from the first and last of the five drafts.

Conclusion

The successive drafts of students' essays provided footprints in the shifting sands of their developing writing strategies. The computer made it easier for students to make these footprints and to preserve them, too. Field notes, analysis notes, conference notes, my notes on their papers, their notes on each others' papers, the other College Writing instructors' notes on their portfolios, and the written comments by the students on their own work were used over time to piece together a partial map to help clarify where these footprints indicate students were coming from and where they may be going in their composing strategies.

"Stentorian Man" began as a piece of writing that characterized many of the problems of text generation that I have associated with the term *micro-voices*. At one level, the piece illustrated how models of writing provided by the students as well as by me in co-creations of curriculum were connected to the students' writing, transforming it so that it reflected the models themselves. A co-created curriculum was also part of the strategy to motivate students to write by incorporating and building on their voices and choices and by efforts to ensure more equality of voice. Investing students as decision makers and contributors was realized in a coaching/collaborating pedagogical style that in this case also employed computer technology in the development of writing skills. I have shown how several features and tools of computers facilitate text generation for my students. Using the computer lab has also enabled students to work at different levels as well as on different assigned projects at their own pace. They were nevertheless all expected to "write like crazy" to get as much writing practice as possible.

The approach, then, attempted to honor individual as well as cultural writing differences. Jerod's love of sports had a place beside Alvin's love of science. Sarah's experimentations with structural metaphors had a place beside Gerald's explorations of grammatical complexity. Amy's emerging feminist consciousness had a place beside Ray's emerging consciousness as an African American man. All these places were linked by issues of youth identity and representation and incorporated into a pedagogy and curriculum characterized by an ability to change and to accommodate change.

In the process, these students actually changed themselves. In various ways and at varying degrees, they broke through their fears of writing and began to see themselves *as* writers; they broke through some of the boundaries of difference and stretched their perceptions to see similarities on the other side; and, they broke through the walls of stentorian sound that surrounded them to find and affirm unique writing voices. Ray ended the last version of his essay with a description of how he had re-visioned the stentorian man. His words, I think, partially reflect these claims.

> Seeing the man again, he was now dressed in a brown leather dinko. His feet were tethered with sandals and in his outstretched hand he carried a spear. His taut body glistened in the sun, and his cacophony transformed into a powerful warrior call. In his woeful song, I heard the voice of mother Africa, calling me home.

4 Changing Classroom Discourse and Culture

The research project under discussion in this chapter focused on a teacher in a San Francisco Bay Area high school. Entitled "African American and Youth Culture as a Bridge to Writing Development," the project, among other things, featured a curricular intervention through which students learned both to critique and to produce popular culture texts along with other literate texts.

I will call that school site Bay View High School. It was an exceptionally prolific source of data for several reasons. First, college students trained by me in two successive courses on issues in secondary English instruction were permitted to observe classes at this site. This experience enabled them to use the skills they had developed in qualitative research techniques of participant/observation, ethnographic interviewing, and notetaking, which included recording systematic descriptions, general descriptions, and analysis notes. My students were thus able to use recently acquired or developed skills to analyze classroom discourse and culture. We ended up with qualitative data for over 600 hours of life and work in classrooms of this school.

The second reason was that this high school had the same diverse demographics as Grand Crossing High School in the Chicago study, which will be discussed in the next chapter. Grand Crossing's student body of approximately 2,000 consisted of more than twenty-one ethnic groups, but the major concentrations were European-, African-, Asian-, and Latino-Americans, with each group making up about 20 percent of the total student body; the additional 20 percent were a mixture of the other groups. Bay View's enrollment of 2,161 students was about 40 percent African American, 30 percent white, 10 percent Asian, 10 percent Latino, and 10 percent other groups; but the majority of this last category were students of mixed race.

This study at Bay View High School investigated how the nature of urban classrooms was changing in response to difference, and how and if educators themselves were effecting change to accommodate difference.

In *Loose Canons*, Henry Louis Gates Jr. (1992) notes:

> Ours is a late twentieth-century world, profoundly fissured by nationality, ethnicity, race, class, and gender. The only way to transcend these divisions is through education that seeks to comprehend diversity. There is no tolerance without respect and no respect without knowledge. Any human being sufficiently curious and motivated can fully possess another culture, no matter how alien it may appear to be. (p. xv)

The possibility of shareable cultural worlds for learning discussed in Chapter 1 was a key premise behind each of my research projects. Therefore, I designed this "African American and Youth Culture" study to build on data from my students' participant/observations, and to further explore ways that teachers were making or could make viable connections between streets and schools—connections between personal/cultural and popular cultural knowledge, on the one hand, and mainstream academic and school knowledge on the other through transformative pedagogy and curriculum.

A third reason this site was extremely valuable was that the woman who became our focal teacher there, whom I will call Ms. Parks, was one of those rare, gifted teachers like Jack MacFarland in *Lives on the Boundary*, who was teaching her heart out and making a real difference in the lives and learning of her students. She came to our attention through the field notes and analysis writings of several of my students, who at different times and for extended periods had done observations in her class. Their reports were so consistently positive and enthusiastic that we (my two graduate researchers and I) arranged to meet and interview her for our project. Ms. Parks had been an English teacher in Bay Area schools for six years. She was a "student" of African American and youth culture and had already made attempts to incorporate both elements into her curriculum and teaching. Ms. Parks's teaching also had been featured prominently throughout a three-hour video documentary, "School Colors," that was done of this high school by Andrews et al. (1994). Andrews and his partners trained the students in video documentary work and clips of the students' work was incorporated into "School Colors." The concomitant filming and broadcasting of this video documentary was a fourth reason this site was particularly fruitful. It provided additional scenes and images of life in this school.

An early, still shot in the film displays the following quotation from the *Brown v. Board of Education* (1954) decision: "It is doubtful that any child may reasonably be expected to succeed in life if he is denied the opportunity of an education. . . . Such an opportunity is a right which must be available to all on equal terms." The film notes that it had been forty years since the Brown decision and twenty-five years since the school district that "Bay View" was part of had voluntarily desegregated its schools, thereby leading the nation in its attempt to achieve total integration in public schools. Forty students, selected to mirror the ethnic diversity of the school, were chosen for a yearlong class in video journalism and trained to produce video tapes to explore the issues of race and ethnicity at Bay View High. It was indicated early in the film why this school was a good site for this exploration. "Today, when large numbers of white students have fled from urban public schools . . . [this school] has maintained as diverse a student body as you can find anywhere. This is the story of a year in the life of a school and its students as they struggle with racial identity and the legacy of school integration. It's a microcosm of America."

The documentary was severely criticized, especially by a number of students for having been edited in such a way as to represent the school as a racial battleground. Critiques flooded the local newspapers and school newspapers, and the film and what it portrayed was the subject of heated debates for several months. I coordinated a forum on the film a few weeks after it aired for faculty and students at our university, bringing people to the discussion, including a former president of the school board, to share their insights with those beyond the lenses of the cameras. Our research also provided significant insights beyond those lenses.

Essentially the film presented a number of powerfully contrasting scenes and images that represented the "legacy of integration" as one that was characterized far more by contestation than cooperation—disdain rather than respect for differences. Scenes of a white male teacher at a nearly all-white class of Advanced Placement British literature were juxtaposed with an African American male teacher with dreadlocked hair teaching a nearly all-black class in African American studies. Images of the all-white cheerleading squad contrasted with images of the all-black pom-pom squad at the same school football games. There were scenes of tracked classes and de-tracked classes. And, there were abundant images of hatred and fear.

The critiques and charges were that the school had been severely misrepresented, that in the hundreds of hours of film shot by the students a very different Bay View existed that was left out or discarded somewhere on the film editor's cutting-room floor. My students were also viewing scenes and images in Bay View's classrooms, but their methods of recording them were through the tools of qualitative research. This chapter joins both of these views in an expanded vision of the school and focuses them on the teaching and learning occurring in Ms. Parks's classes as well as other Bay View teachers' classes to provide insight into some of the provocative issues of changing classroom discourse and culture.

Classroom Discourse

The most fundamental and important functions of schools are achieved through communication. In attempting to discover and describe how the patterns of communicative interactions affected learning in the classrooms we observed at Bay View High, I began with an examination of the nature of classroom discourse as posited by several researchers. Courtney Cazden (1988) notes three of the key reasons why communication is central to educational institutions:

> First, spoken language is the medium by which teaching and learning take place, and in which students demonstrate to teachers much of what they have learned. Second . . . the teacher is responsible for controlling all the talk that occurs while class is officially in session—controlling not just negatively, as a traffic policeman does to avoid collisions, but also positively, to enhance the purposes of education. . . . Third, and perhaps least obviously, spoken language is an important part of the identities of all the participants. (pp. 2–3)

A pervasive feature of "teacher talk" reflects Cazden's second point of control, which is not just the control of talk, but the control of behavior itself. Cazden writes, "Teachers have the right to speak at any time and to any person; they can fill any silence or interrupt any speaker; they can speak to a student anywhere in the room and in any volume or tone of voice. And no one has any right to object" (1988, p. 54). In high schools, this occurs at the very time that students need to master more complicated communication interactions consistent with their increasing age and maturity, yet teachers will sometimes interpret attempts at adultlike communicative behavior as challenges to their own authority. Attempts to transform classroom discourse have been made by changing the locus of control that typically has been an inordinate amount of teacher talk. Teacher-controlled talk requires students to primarily respond to teacher-initiated prompts or questions in order to be evaluated on their mastery of knowledge that the teacher usually already has. But Cazden also mentions a positive feature of the control of discourse, one that enhances learning. In both the Grand Crossing study of the next chapter and the "Micro-Voices" study of the previous one, it was clear that the teacher does not just give over control to the students. Teachers must have significant skill in communication to get students meaningfully involved in discussions as contributors and even as leaders and to broaden the strategies of how they learn.

Joan Cone (1992) has provided one model of how the balance of classroom talk and control of talk can be shifted in favor of students. Essentially, she recognizes the need for students to engage in expansive talk, especially at the beginning of the semester, in order to develop the kinds of relationships that will enhance their working together effectively for the rest of the year. This was especially important, she felt, when she opened the enrollment of her Advance Placement English class to any student in the school who was willing to do the work. But despite innovative teacher/researchers like Cone, the nature of classroom discourse that we observed in many classes at Bay View High reflected the constraining forms of communication and control that Cazden has described and that Goodlad, as discussed earlier in this book, has also documented.

Beyond the issue of control, however, is Cazden's focusing on the fact that the identities of all the participants in classroom communication are intricately tied to the content and structures of the discourse. The communication in the classroom is not only a principal vehicle for learning, it carries cultural cargo as well. Through its official and unofficial discourse the interests, attitudes, obligations, and rights of students and teachers are crystallized in these complex social systems.

In the course of our observations and the collection of data, we focused on trying to answer a number of questions such as the following: What were the different kinds of talk—the different speech events—that made up the communicative ecology of the classroom? Who were the participants? Who were the leaders and who were the listeners in the discussions and why? What were the implicit and explicit rules, codes, and functions of the discourse? To what extent was the IRE (initiation/ response/ evaluation) strategy employed as a structure for classroom discourse? (This kind of talk often takes place in the classroom, where the teacher initiates, the student responds, and the teacher evaluates the response.) What were the strategies of control for the official classroom discourse? What was the nature and extent of unofficial talk by students in the classroom?

Classroom Culture

Additional questions, which focus on the observation of classroom culture and the ways that teachers and students together construct the day-to-day reality of classroom life, come from Collins and Green (1990). In developing a constructivist concept of how meaning is made in classrooms, they note that rather than merely being a room in a place called school, classrooms are defined by the particular ways that the people in them interact over time in attempting to achieve particular educational goals. Their key point is that teachers and students work together to negotiate and build common understandings of what is required to participate in the everyday life of the classroom. Therefore, despite the fact that curricula can be somewhat standardized in schools, classroom life and culture can vary tremendously from class to class as different teachers and different groups of students interact with each other in ways and with motives that may or may not be conscious.

To identify and understand the ways and motives for the co-creations of classroom culture, my study focused on a number of questions. What was the official classroom culture desired by the teacher and what was the unofficial world of peer culture? How did these two worlds intersect? What was the tone or mood of the classroom, and what were the specific factors contributed to creating it? Did the atmosphere of the classroom seem threatening or safe, serious or relaxed, and why? Sizer (1984) describes findings in *Horace's Compromise* that were similar to Goodlad's findings discussed earlier in this book, namely, that one could visit any high school in America and basically observe the same processes in the classroom. So, this study considered the ways the classes observed mirrored this comment, or the ways they were able to break out of this mode of what Sizer calls "mediocre sameness."

A final consideration was the design and physical structure of the classrooms observed to determine if they facilitated or impeded the processes of teaching and learning. This included taking account of any technology that existed in the classroom and the uses made of it. Therefore, the classroom discourse and culture were assessed in terms of how they interacted with and were revealed in the curriculum content, pedagogical styles and strategies, assessment practices, and the design and physical structures of the classroom.

Institutional structures also contribute to the nature of classroom discourse and culture, and one structure that has had a profound effect on general school culture and the specific cultures of individual classes is the system of tracking. At Bay View, the highest tracks of Advance Placement (A.P.) classes were 85 percent white and Asian. This was in stark contrast to the low-track courses. They were also sharply contrasted in terms of the kinds of students in the African American studies courses which, though not a track defined by academic ability, had 85 percent black students.

The issues of tracking are especially charged because significant research has shown their detrimental consequences for certain populations of public school students—especially African American students—who are disproportionately represented in low skilled vocational tracks and ability groupings (Oakes, 1985). African American students are also far more likely than whites to be placed in special education programs and to be labeled mentally retarded (Lomotey, 1990). Added to this, African American students are suspended three times as frequently as whites and they comprise 40 percent of all students suspended or expelled (Reed, 1988).

Students at Bay View High may not have been able to quote the statistics, but at varying levels they were aware of the differential attitudes, opportunities, and patterns of treatment experienced by different groups of students, and they knew that these issues were linked to the problems of segregation and confrontation that the editors of the documentary had decided to make their central focus in representing the culture of specific classrooms and of the school generally. Despite the real problems that many people had with the film, I feel it did provide some insights into life in an urban, multicultural school environment by highlighting some of the most dramatic and difficult issues in education today. Perceptions of students, teachers, administrators, and parents were revealed in the film regarding the system of tracking, and these perceptions offered one starting point for changing school culture.

According to one African American male student who was interviewed by the video journalists, "'Bay View' is like the real world, and the real world is totally segregated. There's no such thing as integration when it comes to America. We all want to be with our own, and that's the way humans are." A white female student responded to this issue by saying, "I think it has to do with tracking. Because if people are not integrated in the classes, then they are not going to meet each other." Interestingly, at a later point in the film, the same African American student mentioned above made a further comment that was similar to the sentiments of this female student when he also noted, "I think that the reason we're segregated during lunch and after school and all that is because we don't have classes together. How can we interact if we don't have classes together."

The teachers shown in the film had strong opinions on this issue too. A white female teacher whose scenes on the film showed her doing a phenomenal job of teaching in one of the new de-tracked freshman classes noted, "If I teach a heterogeneous classroom where these students are brought in to be a part of the group, they are going to do a hell of a lot better than if you segregate them, tell them that they're stupid, put them in a lower level. And that's effectively what you're doing if you put them in a lower level is saying . . . you can't hack it in the real world." On the other hand, a white male teacher who also taught a de-tracked English class was skeptical. He had the following comments on the de-tracking initiative:

> You can have different groups working on different projects. You
> know, maybe the enrichment kids are doing one thing and the kids

who are just getting their basic skills are doing another activity, but that's basically just segregation within the classroom. I've had the higher skill kids complain more than once, saying, you know, 'I'm tired of being the teacher. We want to learn. We want you to be our teacher.' To keep all of the students engaged, I as a teacher would have to come in with three or four lesson plans. And to be quite honest, I'm not willing to do that every day. I'm a public high school teacher. I don't think I'm supposed to be a saint or a martyr. I want to be a good teacher, but I think that most days, I should have to come in with one lesson plan.

The de-tracking initiative was a bold move on the part of the administrators and faculty at Bay View. It was seen, first and foremost, as a way of increasing the achievement and retention of underachieving students. It was also designed to transform some of the institutionally structured differences between students and to mitigate their differential treatment while providing classroom environments that allowed for real cross-cultural interactions and learning among the various groups of students at the school.

There was a complex history of the struggle to institute de-tracking at Bay View. A school administrator had analyzed the D and F rates of students in lower-track classes. One of the original goals in creating the lower tracks was to serve under-achieving students by putting them into classes where the range of abilities was smaller, and where students could receive instruction and could work with curriculum materials that were more closely matched to their ability levels. But after years of ability grouping, the data on these students showed that they were not increasing their achievement. The ability groupings were just not working the way it was argued that they would, and the problem was compounded by statistics showing that 66 percent of African American students who entered the school as freshmen would eventually disappear at some point during the four years of high school and not graduate. At the same time, it was noticed that in the history department's experimentation with de-tracking, D and F rates had gone down for students who otherwise were locked in lower tracks. The math department was also doing a kind of de-tracking by compressing the number of tracks in its course offerings.

Still, a number of factors had to come together for the school to move toward de-tracking. A new principal came in with a mandate from the superintendent to do something to change the D and F rates and to improve student retention and achievement. Also, a number of older teachers were retiring, making it possible for fifty-nine new teachers to be hired during this phase. Incentives were provided for the history department and the English department to work together on implementing a pilot program of de-tracked classes. Flurries of meetings were constantly being held with and among teachers, parents, and administrators. There were a number of unsung heroes who put in long hours to facilitate this process.

In the 1992–93 school year, a modest pilot with four freshman courses was initiated. Even then, two of the teachers working with pilot classes quit the program in midyear. Yet a basis had been established and the results were encouraging enough for de-tracked classes to be increased across the ninth grade in the next academic year with the aim that when these students become sophomores, their tenth-grade classes would also be de-tracked. The pattern was to continue until graduation so that eventually the whole school would be de-tracked.

Armed with focus questions and qualitative recording techniques, we were able to capture some of the real-life, day-to-day activities and interactions of teachers and students in school. In our data we saw patterns for some of the possibilities and problems of educational change.

Problems of Changing Classroom Discourse and Culture

In one sense of the term, discourse and culture in America's classrooms are dramatically changing independent of the initiatives of educators. One aspect of this change, alluded to in the introduction of this book, was a sense that the contemporary rhythms of student learning were somehow out of sync with the cadence of teaching for many teachers. The school-place has necessarily changed through changes in the nature of the student populations that comprise public schools. But school change has been structural as well as cultural. The political, economic, technological, and institutional environment in which schooling takes place has also changed and effected change in schools.

One change that is upsetting to many teachers is the extent to which the school knowledge they have been positioned and sanctioned to teach is being questioned, resisted, or even rejected by some of their students. A critique of this issues was presented in Chapter 1, using the contrasting perspectives of Fordham and Ogbu on the one hand and Alpert on the other. The question was whether the very culture itself of some youth, particularly African Americans, was oppositional to the culture of schools, or whether it was possible that they were resisting specific ways of teaching as well as specific kinds of curricular content. The classroom discourse and culture revealed in the data from this study as well as in the documentary provided opportunities to further consider ways that school life and learning were both accepted and resisted.

One provocative example from the film and one from our data will be used to illustrate the changing discourse and culture at Bay View that was sometimes revealed in acts, often speech acts, of resistance and acceptance. These acts were framed and defined by issues that were cultural, like identity, and issues that were structural, like tracking. In the first example, a group of students were engaged in a heated discussion in a classroom after the class had ended. There was an African American male and female, a Latino male, and two white males. Their physical positions in relationship to each other during the discussion actually altered to reflect the contrasting positions on identity that they were contending.

> *Latino student:* The psychological effects of slavery, the legacy of slavery is still with us today.
>
> *White student:* Yeah, I know you don't agree with me on this, but are we all Americans?
>
> *Latino student:* No.
>
> *White student:* No, why?
>
> *Latino student:* I don't consider myself an American.
>
> *White student:* But why. I'm a first, I'm not even a first generation [American]. I don't look at America as if it's white America. No, it's all of us. There was slavery at one time, but . . .
>
> *Black female student:* But all of us do not survive successfully in this society. Listen, when the government looks at me, they don't look at me as an American. They look at the Africa in me.
>
> *Other white student:* You're still an American. You can't get away from that.
>
> *Latino student:* Please. Don't define me. You've defined me too long.
>
> *Other white student:* I defined you?
>
> *Latino student:* Yeah. You just called me an American. Please. I take that as a insult.

The separate ways that these students conceived of themselves relative to a fundamental concept of identity, the idea of citizenship, the idea of belonging—or of not belonging—provide a potent text and texture to their motives both of resistance and acceptance. The two white students are able to affirm their sense of belonging, though one's family has not been in America very long, and they don't see why that same sense of belonging should not be shared by the students of color. The students of color provided a little of the texture for why they could not in good conscience embrace an identity of being American. The female student touched on the reality of the differential treatment and opportunities of some groups in America, and further noted that the government itself diminishes any sense of belonging to America—"they don't look at me as an American. They look at the Africa in me."

Clearly, the resistance of these students of color to identifying themselves as American and their sense of not belonging is deeply felt. It was epitomized in the statement of the Latino student who said that being called an American by the white student was an insult. The white students' acceptance of their identification with and sense of belonging to America seemed equally strong. These kinds of differing perceptions of who they are and what their relationships are to the state, to the government, to local communities, to the school, to teachers and administrators, and to each other as students are part of the uneven landscape on which lines of contestation are drawn and across which different groups snipe at each other from the trenches of hatred and fear.

Interestingly, in the documentary and in American society, the feelings of hatred are most often associated with the people the society itself has marginalized, whereas the feelings of fear are almost always attributed to people for whom the society has "privileged" with opportunities and allowed or created a sense of inclusion. The bitter animosity and hostility that some people of color are perceived as having is in the family of oppositional behaviors that Ogbu feels characterizes the collective/social identity of people he has termed "involuntary minorities." Fear, on the other hand—the feelings of apprehension and anxiety caused by the presence or imminence of danger—is a natural human response to the hatred that people of color are now presumed to have. Actually, as Ms. Parks who is one of the English teachers at Bay View perceptively suggests, African American students are often in the grip of fear themselves, which comes from a number of sources in the school and in their lives.

One problem with this formulation is that historically and contemporarily in America, it has been the hatred and racism of some of the white people in power that has worked to reject and obstruct (often violently) the desires and pathways that African Americans and other groups have attempted to pursue to gain full inclusion into America's work places, communities, schools, and other institutions. Blacks have defined themselves as African Americans, but as the student noted, America seems to focus on the African and not the American component of that identity through its methods of simultaneously highlighting and marginalizing difference.

The history of blacks in America prolifically reveals that in every period the dominant motive of the majority of African Americans was toward inclusion in this country rather than exclusion and that the various movements toward separation on the part of blacks did not themselves turn merely on an oppositional identity. In other words, to characterize a group of people as having an oppositional collective and social identity (even though oppositional behaviors have been and will continue to be one form of a range of efforts to resist oppression) is to miss the most central motives revealed in the history and struggle of African Americans in this country. More accurately, an oppositional identity better characterizes white America to the extent that it has historically and contemporarily erected a myriad barriers to inclusion through its power structures and social practices.

The attitudes of these students of color are grounded in the realities of school life. They see themselves often being forced to learn about things they have no interest in and penalized for things they do want to learn. In the film one of the teachers in the African American Studies department noted, "Many of the students who do not see themselves in the material end up getting kicked out of school because they don't attend class, because they're not interested. They get F's on their tests because they're not interested. It's not that they can't study; it's like, they look at the material and say, why do I want to study that." The department gets criticism for offering classes with an intensive focus in black history, literature, and culture, while classes like A.P. British literature, which also have an exclusive focus, are not seen as essentially the same thing. The teacher of A.P. British literature noted on the video:

> I enjoy teaching this class because I think some of the better intellectual discussions in the high school go on here. It doesn't attract a diversity or a wide diversity of students. I think that the authors that we read, because they are all white, tend to alienate some of the nonwhite kids. I should probably go around to bright kids of the other ethnicities and say, you know, I'd really like you in my class. But, I'd also have to convince them why they should spend the whole semester studying writers from one country.

Ms. Jackson's Class

From the qualitative data we developed more than fifty descriptive/analyses of separate, extended observations of teaching and learning at Bay View. Each one contributed a piece to the mosaic of settings, actions, dialogues, and people in the school life of Bay View. A profile of one of these cases, featuring two classes taught by the same teacher, revealed how the nature and motives of both resistance and acceptance crystallize in the system of tracking, and as such it provides more understanding of why there is such a crucial need to change this system. It also graphically shows how the nature of classroom discourse and culture are tied to the meanings enacted by a particular teacher and class.

Ms. Jackson was a strong-willed, African American woman who was approaching retirement as a teacher at Bay View. Though the observation was scheduled to be of her ethnic literature class, she requested that it be extended to her world literature class also. She mentioned that the ethnic literature class was a lower-track class, while the world literature was a higher-track class. The ethnic studies class was not a part of the African American Studies department course offerings, but along with the world literature class it was offered by the English department.

During the five weeks that we observed the ethnic literature class, the attendance was extremely low, ranging from about three-quarters of the students on a good day to about half the students on other days. Most of the students were African American and Latino, and there were two white students. The class was completely disengaged from learning. At any point during the class, half of the students would have their heads on their tables. Some slept through the whole period, and amazingly, actually snored. There was something else odd about the culture of the classroom; the students didn't seem to really know each other. They referred to each other as "that boy," or "what's her name," or "that white guy with the purple hair." Clearly, they did not share a sense of community or see themselves as a unit of any kind. Class was merely a placeholder in their lives, taking up an hour of their day at school. When interviewed, Ms. Jackson noted that her aims in this class were to prepare some of the better students in the class for the higher-track world literature classes and to teach the class how to take notes after reading the chapters.

The contrasts between this class and her world literature class were apparent as soon as the world literature students walked through the door. The noticeable thing was their enthusiasm; they were much more excited about coming to class. The class was just about evenly split between black and white students, with a sprinkling of Latino and Asian students. The students worked more as a collective unit, encouraging each other to attend and to be on time. Overall, the students respected and even admired Ms. Jackson. She was like a mother/grandmother figure to them. They submitted to her authority and responded to her teaching methods, which were primarily traditional with lots of "frontal" instruction. Ms. Jackson, too, responded to them very differently than she did to her students in the ethnic literature class. If a student walked into class a little sluggishly, she would automatically pull the student to the side and check to see if anything was wrong. On the first day of observation, she was serving warm bread to her students as a reward for their perfect attendance.

The assigned reading in the world literature class for part of the observation period was *The Color Purple*. Ms. Jackson began each class with a fifteen-minute in-class writing assignment on the previous day's reading homework, centered around questions designed to reveal the students' grasp of the key issues and themes in the book. The questions directed students to issues such as patriarchy, the varieties of love, the roles that writing and education played in the book. The writing was also designed to prepare the students to think through the issues in writing as "springboards" for discussion. The students interviewed liked the fact that Ms. Jackson made these efforts to engage them in the readings, which they said they were enjoying.

However, students also felt that sometimes the discussions were flat. Some expressed a desire to explore issues in longer essays. Some wanted to discuss the novel in small groups. They also complained that the work was sometimes too easy. But they did not feel that they could ask Ms. Jackson to change her teaching methods. One of the reasons they were in a "higher" track was that they had learned to accept their roles as obedient students who did not question the teacher's authority.

On the other hand, many students who ended up in the other track (the ethnic literature class) were there for reasons associated with the history of their behavior as much as for their perceived lack of ability. The assigned reading in the ethnic literature class during the observation was *To Kill a Mockingbird*. Ms. Jackson began each class by asking if students had done their homework. The same three students in the class were the only ones who ever actually did the work. But the routine was consistent. She would praise the three who did do their homework and would remind the class that these would be the students moving up into higher tracks. Everyone else would get zeros. Unfortunately, attempting to do the work did not really help those few students to fare much better in the class. One African American female student who was interviewed was clearly as articulate and perceptive as any of the students in world literature. Yet, she believed she had been placed in the lower-track class because she "was quiet" and extremely shy in class. However, in the one-on-one interview, she had no qualms about voicing her insightful opinions. When she complained to Ms. Jackson about receiving C's and D's in the class because she felt her efforts were worthy of B's or better, she was told that she would be getting B pluses if she spoke more in class. Yet Ms. Jackson never called on her, even though she often called on disengaged or disruptive students to keep control of the class; she even gave them grades for attempting to discuss the work and to thus make up for the work they had not done at home.

Every day, students either read aloud in class for the whole period, or Ms. Jackson solicited oral plot summaries from a couple of the students who had done their homework. In interviews, the students articulated the fact that they were not only unmotivated but also unchallenged. Tragically, the nature of student resistance—revealed in constant and often verbally aggressive disruptions—suggested (and confirmed by some students) that they were misbehaving in direct response to the boredom they were experiencing. At times, they were being disruptive to make the class more interesting. Things would get unbelievably caustic. Students made fun of what Ms. Jackson wore; they made senior citizen jokes that were audible to her and other class members; they cursed, and even cursed at Ms. Jackson. One student rudely challenged her, "I don't have to respect you, 'cause you got to earn my respect . . . and even if you wanted to shut me up, you'd have to make me . . . and you can't even do that much." The shy student talked about how sad and ashamed she was by the behavior of her classmates and how sorry she felt for Ms. Jackson. But Ms. Jackson had decided to just "put up with this disrespect" and to try and ignore the disruptions until she could finally move on—into retirement.

If Ms. Jackson's ethnic literature class was an isolated example of a class from hell, it would be pointless to examine it to see what could be learned. The fact is, however, that far too many classrooms are hostile places where neither teachers nor students feel safe or welcome; where the discourse is acerbic and insolent, and the culture is corrosive and dispiriting. These problems were no less intense simply because the ethnic background of the teacher matched the ethnic background of the majority of her students. The situation highlights, once again, the contrastive nature of adult versus youth culture and reinforces the need for teachers to employ methods that connect with youth in ways that encompass their interests and experiences as well as some of the problems that they bring to class. The situation was also no less intense because the teacher was an experienced teacher. Clearly new technologies of instruction are needed to keep time with the different rhythms of learning. In other words, despite the match of the ethnicity of the teacher and despite her ability to be more successful with other groups of students, the extreme resistance that characterized her ethnic studies class was predicated on the actual nature of pedagogy and curriculum to which they were exposed.

From the corpus of data, it is also clear that, though it was a more extreme example, Ms. Jackson's ethnic literature class mirrored a number of the problems that stem from consciously created, institutional structures of schooling and that interact with and influence pedagogy and curriculum. Tracking is a structure that has been so deeply embedded in education that its real effects have not been rigorously questioned until lately. It is now being seen as having devastating consequences for a host of issues tied to effective learning, such as motivation, self-esteem, discipline, cooperation, respect for others, and a sense of the school as a community.

The problems of tracking loomed even larger in our data when we were able to compare the same teachers teaching in different tracks. It was truly amazing how consistently the field notes indicated situations like the following:

> There were real differences in the way [the teacher] approached the two classes. His energy level and excitement decreased in the lower track. He yelled more. The frustration on his face was obvious. He admitted that teaching his lower-track class was something he did not look forward to. The students clearly picked up on the negative energy of the teacher and the never ending cycle of clashes continued.

Tracking in courses like the ethnic and world literature classes influenced how the teacher perceived students, how students perceived the teacher, and how students and the teacher perceived themselves. Interviews with these students showed that they were aware of how they have been tracked in English. The "lower-track" student revealed being with basically the same groups of students in English classes for the past three years. It was difficult to ever get out of the track in which one was placed. Once they had been determined as tracks, the course names "hooked" onto the classes were irrelevant. Curriculum was not the determining factor either. For example, *The Color Purple* was part of the curriculum of world literature while *To Kill a Mockingbird* found its way into ethnic literature. But beyond the actual curriculum and the constraints of the system of tracking in Ms. Jackson's classroom, the attitude and expectations that the teacher had for students also had an important effect.

In order to learn, students must use what they already know to give meaning to what the teacher presents to them. But this possibility depends on the social relationships revealed in classroom culture and the communication system inherent in the patterns and motives of discourse that teachers must initiate but collaboratively establish with the students in the intersections of teaching and learning.

Possibilities for Changing Classroom Discourse and Culture

At Bay View, the problems were intense, but the possibilities for effectively changing the nature of schooling were also being dramatically demonstrated. One of the cases in the data was a young white woman teacher who had been one of the fifty-nine new teachers hired as the school began to transform its tracking system. Our observations and analyses confirmed and extended our understanding of certain aspects of pedagogical and curricular change that were evident in her teaching. She was the teacher quoted earlier in this chapter affirming the value of heterogeneous grouping, and her own words do the best job of characterizing her curriculum and instruction strategies:

> You must make a kid believe that he can do anything in order for them to achieve. You won't do that if you put them into a track. You take the gas right out of them. "Pablo" is really smart. "Pablo" slides by. "Pablo" doesn't know how to challenge himself. But, if we have a research project like this one we just did, he's responsible for research, and critical thinking, and working with others, which he's not so good at. And that is where you get "Pablo" to challenge himself and work hard because he had to try really hard to work with "Nathan," not to be arrogant, and also pull him in. And he did it! "Nathan" learned something, and therefore was able to tell people what he learned. He was really able to say this is going on in this part of the world. This is the problem; and this is why; and this is what I think we should do to solve it. He contributed. So, when people say to me, I'm worried that my kid is not going to be challenged in a heterogeneous classroom, my response is how can they not be because what we're doing is not easy. What we're doing is challenging kids to really look within themselves and grow.

Our data showed that this teacher's words were not just a reflection of general hopes for success with heterogeneous groupings. Students were being motivated and challenged in her classes; discipline problems were minimal; and there was a strong, productive sense of class community. In one instructive scene in the documentary, she is shown in a conference with Nathan who physically is a tower next to her, and she discovers while talking to him that he has a set of dice. When she asks what he is doing with these, Nathan says, "Shooting them." She asks him to give her the dice, and he complies but says he has to have them back because they belong to a friend. Her response is to tell Nathan to go and come back with a book in order to continue the conference, which he does.

Nathan was the kind of student who could have been hostile if he had chosen to. He could easily have become part of the 66 percent of black students who used to start school at Bay View, but would never finish there. But something was going on in this class that was encouraging him to develop as a learner and in the process to change the way he viewed both himself and school. His potential transformation through learning was tied to the fact that his interest was captured and his experience was acknowledged in the content of his learning, which took place in a supportive but challenging classroom environment to which his contributions were valued.

Ms. Parks's Class

Cases of transformative pedagogical and curriculum strategies were revealed in the data alongside cases of more traditional approaches to instruction. The last case that I will use in this chapter is of Ms. Parks, who was the focal teacher relative to the curriculum intervention that was part of our study at this school. Ms. Parks is a vivacious, assertive woman who has a dynamic teaching style. Her classes were prominently displayed throughout the documentary, and after it aired, she started getting calls at the school from teachers all over the country praising her work and requesting advice about teaching. On the film she notes, "I got into teaching because I saw what was happening in the school system, and it was appalling to me that many students were having continual conflict in the school system, and I thought I could do something about that." She has taught for about six years, and before coming to Bay View she taught in an alternative high school in Oakland for students who had dropped out of regular high school. She doesn't think tracking works generally, though she notes that there are different kinds of tracking, consequently there are times when it might work to a degree. But the key problem, she feels, with contemporary tracking systems is the differing expectations by teachers for the students in different tracks. She also argues that today's curriculum does not allow teachers to teach the students what they need to know to survive in life.

Ms. Parks's classroom does not reveal itself as an English class in terms of its decor. There are a few posters around, but they depict images that would more likely be found on the walls of a teenager's room. Notes on the chalkboard announce events taking place at the school or other items of interest for the students. One note, for example, stated that a female student had been sexually assaulted on the school's campus during October, and it advised students to be cautious. What decor there was reflected the interests of the students more so than that of the teacher.

Ms. Parks is a caring teacher who has worked hard at establishing and maintaining relationships with her students through a variety of rituals that the students seem to appreciate. When students filed into class, she was at the door to greet them with small talk, a pat on the shoulder, a cheerful smile. She would also joke with her students at times and even engage in a brief turn of signifying. Once a student walked into class and said, "Hey, Ms. Parks, why don't you do something with that hair." She quickly retorted, "Why don't you do something with your face." They both laughed.

When class started, she often shifted immediately into a high-keyed, animated, direct style that is characteristic of modes of black discourse, a style that is dialogic and receiver-centered and thereby encourages exchange. She diligently shaped her lessons to promote extensive student communication and discussion. Students worked in groups daily, but there were also times when they were arranged into one large circle. Her voice was heard less than half of the time. The rest of the time, a succession of individual voices, or a medley of many voices were heard as students tried to put their ideas and feelings about the readings into their own words. She moved the discussion in a way designed to reach each student, and she was usually able to address each student two or three times during the period, whether it was to ask an academic question or to make a social comment or to give a reprimand. In fact, she had no problems blending social talk and academic talk.

Ms. Parks encouraged her students to think, and she believed that their thinking should be revealed in their class participation, though she knew some students were reluctant to participate. She would stress to her students that she herself was not perfect in attempting to get them to overcome their fears in speaking before the class and in representing their ideas. She often assigned topics that her students had to make a presentation on in class to make their learning active and performative. At times the tone of the classroom was almost overwhelming, but Ms. Parks always looked at ease, and she was clearly in control. Through both her language and her behavior she communicated that she took the students and herself seriously. She made them feel that their ideas were important and encouraged their expression.

Ms. Parks gave a lot of homework. She set her class expectations high and motivated her students to strive to reach them despite the fact that they would sometimes ask to be assigned fewer books to read or request less homework. She quizzed students on the readings, but she did not grade them by the number of right and wrong answers to questions. Instead she had them write their responses to issues and themes in the book. Her grading methods are also interesting in other ways. She allowed students to retake quizzes they did poorly on because they may not have thoroughly done the readings. By allowing students to reread the chapter and take the test again, she was giving them the opportunity to decide if they wanted to work hard enough to get an A.

In discussing the readings, Ms. Parks would lead her students through explorations of sophisticated and subtle themes. And when they wrote about these themes, she was not concerned if their opinions were starkly different from hers as long as they provided enough evidence to support their views. She wanted them both to understand the story and to find something interesting to write about. But she would often write detailed comments on their papers. She also had her students write three drafts before they turned in the final version of the paper. She wanted her students to be sensitive to the mechanics of their papers, but her major focus was on the gradual improvement of their writing style, which was the main determinant of their grades on the essays.

A look at Ms. Parks in action in the classroom reveals why people were calling and writing the school from all over the country to praise her work. The documentary showed a couple of scenes from one of her freshman classes that illustrated how Ms. Parks was able to effectively get her students to think and learn. This was not one of the initial classes to be de-tracked in the school, so its composition was pretty much homogenous both in ethnicity and skills level. In two or three years, these students would have eventually ended up in an ethnic literature class like the one that Ms. Jackson was teaching if in fact they had been able to stay successfully in school at all. They came to Ms. Parks's class with all the "dog-ate-my-homework" or more recently "the-computer-crashed-with-my-homework-on-it" excuses students are capable of. Ms. Parks, however, would admonish them for their attempts to self-destruct just as readily as she would praise them for their successes and earnest attempts to achieve as in the following example:

> *Ms. Parks:* Reggie, with no book, no pen, no paper. What do you want to learn in this class.
>
> *Reggie:* It's all in my head.
>
> *Ms. Parks:* Uh huh.
>
> *Reggie:* It is. Well, whatever you're going to teach, I want to learn it.
>
> *Ms. Parks:* How are you going to learn it?
>
> *Reggie:* By the way you are going to teach it.

At this point Ms. Parks launched into the following mini-lecture challenging Reggie's attitude, with obvious implications for the other students in the class.

> This class does not work, this school does not work, your lives do not work if you don't, number one, respect yourselves and, number two, respect each other. We're sitting here trying to talk about change and how to make a plan for how to make something work in your lives, and you guys are sitting here spending more time putting each other down, and being rude, and disrespecting yourselves, than you are working on how to make your life work. Now you can do that for the rest of your lives but you won't pass a class, and you won't get a job, and you won't have a house, and you won't have a bank account, and you won't drive a car, and you won't have a family that respects you, and you won't raise children that will graduate from high school. And the system that you are a part of will continue to stay in the circular motion that it's in, and nothing will ever change. So make a decision.

Ms. Parks understood, however, that her students were struggling to manage a number of situations in their lives that created real obstacles to their being open and willing to engage in learning in school. They were sensitive to the differential ways that they have been treated in schools and in the society at large, and they often reserved their trust and commitment to a system that had not served them well. Rather than ignore the complicated issues that her students were confronting in their lives, Ms. Parks's technique of blending academic talk with social talk in the classroom helped students externalize and attempt to understand their life experiences. She connected these experiences to vital aspects of their work in school rather than rejecting them. Ms. Parks engaged in a style of receiver-centered classroom discourse that in its structure and in its openness to topics allowed for a wide array of student voices and student issues to be heard. Students were able to initiate topics and take more turns to talk on them; and through the discussions they were able to use the classroom as one vantage point from which to view the world in which they lived. In this regard Ms. Parks noted:

> One of the things I found that's really successful in dealing with, you know, that dynamic that these two sides are almost fighting each other to survive with fear in white America and anger in black America is letting them talk about it. This school has got to engage in discussion where kids feel safe and where they can learn from each other.

The following example from the documentary typifies some of the discussions in which the students gave reasons for consciously exhibiting behaviors and projecting themselves in ways that would intimidate other groups. After stating a couple examples of these tactics, one student went on to express the following thoughts:

> *Student:* I don't hate white people; I just hate what they did to my race, the way they tried to destroy our race.
>
> *Ms. Parks:* Why do you feel that you still need to keep saying that we are oppressed from slavery? As many generations as you are away from slavery, why do you feel, or what's happening in your life that's making you feel that way? Is it something at school?
>
> *Student:* No, it's not something at school. But, it's everything I see in everyday life. That everyday slave mentality.

Another student in the class provided an example of "that everyday slave mentality" by recounting his experience when the school's basketball team went to play another team that was in the suburbs. On the way home after the game, he and a few of his team members stopped at a minimart to get a snack. A white woman went out of her way to stop her car and come over and ask them what gang they belonged to. This scene echoes the one I noted earlier regarding my college writing students: a woman called the student newspaper to complain that the students were pictured flashing gang signs in the paper, when actually the four fingers they held up indicated that they were in the freshman recruiting class of 1994.

Ms. Parks acknowledged the validity of her students' experiences with stereotyping, but continued to press for what in their specific school experiences was impeding their achievement in school. She helped them to objectify their experiences and examine them as part of the process of setting goals for their lives as well as setting goals for themselves in school. Ms. Parks did not deny the reality of what her students were feeling, but she also, perceptively, saw that in addition to their anger they carried a lot of fear and anxiety themselves. This was reflected in her comments in a parent/teacher conference regarding the low achievement of one of her students.

> "Troy" is a very bright student who is so angry. But more than anger, what I see in "Troy" is fear. And that fear is about not really believing he can succeed. He, like many other students, is not sure what succeeding means. "Troy" is a piece of the future. If he fails, then the society fails because for every student that doesn't make it, there's somebody out there to rob you; there's somebody out there to rape you, there's somebody out there that we in the society who are working have to pay for. These kids that don't graduate, don't go away. And until society recognizes that, then nothing is going to change. . . . If Troy didn't want to be successful at something in his life he wouldn't keep coming to school.

Ms. Parks's students live with fear and danger in their lives outside of school, but they also experience a more subtle fear inside school from dangers that they sense but are often not able to articulate. They are in danger of being misperceived and stereotyped as being dumb or violent. They are in danger of being misevaluated and placed in tracks that don't go anywhere. They are in danger of slipping through the seams of society as well as being caught in its zippers, and ending up in hospitals, mental institutions, prisons, graves. In *The Joy Luck Club* when the situations were desperate, people were able to take joy in the hope that things would eventually change. These students are in danger of losing hope. This is the nihilistic threat that Cornel West (1993a; 1993b) talks about in his speeches and writings that gives rise to a numbing detachment and destructive anger that gets directed both inward and outward as one of the consequences of failed potential.

By changing classroom discourse and culture to be more reflective of her students' needs, Ms. Parks effectively helped her students to realize their potential: they were able to recognize it and to bring it into existence. The students needed to see some of their own images and interests reflected in the material they were expected to learn, and Ms. Parks did this and also powerfully blended aspects of social and academic talk. She extended her teaching to address some of the things they needed to know to survive in life. They needed to belong and feel that they were a part of a community of learners, and Ms. Parks worked to create an environment of fairness and caring, but also of high expectations and challenge. She successfully exploited technologies of instruction that incorporated the students' rhythms of learning, developing their skills for accessing and displaying information; she helped her students learn how to want to learn. In essence, their experiences in the discourse and culture of the Ms. Parks's classroom addressed their needs for personal and cultural representation in the acts and facts of schooling. She designed ways to integrate and build on connections between their personal/cultural knowledge and school knowledge; she provided ways for them to apprehend and express that knowledge through learning strategies that were active and performative; and, she found ways to excite and motivate their learning to increase their desire to achieve.

After the documentary aired, Ms. Parks not only received a slew of calls and letters at the school. She also mentioned in one of the meetings on our project that thirty or forty people whom she didn't know, in addition to a number of parents of students in the school, came by the school to meet and congratulate her on her teaching. Some just wanted to give her a hug and say thanks. But everyone wanted to know how she did such a good job with her students; they wanted to know her teaching strategy. Ms. Parks tells them that she has a plan for what she wants her students to achieve each day but that her main goals for them are more global. Consequently, she feels she can instantly alter her daily plans to address the immediate dynamics of her classrooms in ways that still move her students in the ultimate direction of her goals. She wants her students to develop skills and behaviors that will make them viable in the world, but she wants those skills to extend to their being able to decode the world and their relationships to it. She tries to make her students realize that they can't change the world without changing themselves.

Culture and Curriculum

In addition to the ways Ms. Parks had already designed her teaching for motivating and challenging her students, she also decided to work with my project for the development of a curricular intervention that attempts to tap directly into students' backgrounds and interests to see how that might help stimulate learning generally and improve their writing specifically. Consequently, we implemented a very specific way to change classroom discourse and culture. This project's formulation along with the early responses of the students is significant to the overall discussion of meaningful ways of changing classroom discourse and culture in schools.

It was noticed in many of the classroom observations how student discourse revealed significant influences from African American modes and styles of expression and from cultural sources like rap and hip-hop music as well as sports. These cultural sources also influence aspects of youth culture generally. It was noted that around 75 percent of the students in the school consciously used elements of vocabulary, grammar, and style associated with these black cultural sources. Some used it more than others. For example, Latinos used it more than whites, who in turn used it more than Asians, and black students themselves used it to varying degrees.

We decided to build on elements of African American and youth culture generally, giving a specific focus to music, especially some of the positive aspects of rap music relative to its thematic content, its critical voice, and its oral and written styles and performances. Cornel West (1993b, p. 65) notes that some rap artists "attempt to do what I attempt to do, as a public intellectual. And that is, to tell the truth. . . . There's no doubt that there's a very, very powerful critique of white supremacy in the work." According to Catherine Tabb Powell (1991):

> [Rap] . . . emerged from the streets of inner-city neighborhoods as a genuine reflection of the hopes, concerns, and aspirations of urban Black youth in this, the last quarter of the 20th century. . . . [R]ap is part of a tradition of oral recitation that originated in Africa many centuries ago. This tradition is exemplified by the West African griot, or troubadour/storyteller. To the accompaniment of drums or other percussive instruments, griots entertain and educate their audiences by reciting tribal history and current events. (p. 245)

Although some rap artists use explicit language and sometimes incorporate images that denigrate women particularly, our intention was not to use the actual music in class or in any way reinforce negative images. Rather, background research for the study showed that there was so much being written about the artists, issues, aesthetics, performances, etc. of rap music and culture, that the entire intervention could be based on this overwhelming body of text-based material without necessarily using actual rap songs and videos in the classes. The hypothesis was that these texts could be used as a bridge to give explicit models and motivation for students to further develop critical thinking and writing skills. There are a number of studies that document successful strategies for incorporating and building on elements of African American culture to facilitate learning and literacy development in school settings (Brooks, 1985; Delain, Pearson, & Anderson, 1985; Delpit, 1990; Gee, 1989; Heath & Branscombe, 1985; Ladson-Billings, 1990; Lee, 1991). In particular, the work of Carol Lee (1991) has demonstrated the success of a strategy for using signifying structures in African American language to effect a pedagogical scaffolding that helps readers develop skills in literary analysis. Lee argues that the pedagogical potential of the way "culture and cognition 'co-construct' one another . . . can be viewed in Vygotskian terms as cross-fertilization of scientific and spontaneous concepts" (p. 293). She notes that research has provided "meaningful insights into the texture and nuances of the interplay of culture and cognition . . . but [suggests that] what is missing . . . in terms of enriching the links between everyday practice and schooling are specific descriptions of the knowledge structures taught in school as they relate to the knowledge structures constructed within non-school social settings" (pp. 292–293).

Lee has developed strategies for using signifying and other rhetorical devices that characterize what Zora Neale Hurston originally termed "speakerly" texts to help African American students link oral talk to literary language and critique. Her research was especially consistent with and useful to the formulation of our project, which draws on the familiarity and competence that many African American students and other students have with aspects of rap music and culture, recognizing them as a bridge into higher-order thinking and the production of more sophisticated writing texts.

This curriculum intervention began by creating a questionnaire for the students in the two junior classes selected by each of our focal teachers. The questionnaires helped determine what levels and kinds of adaptive or spontaneously developed competence these high school students had relative to rap music and culture. The questionnaires were also the initial part of our efforts to incorporate student input into curriculum choices of issues, themes, and forms of cultural production. Their responses, in conjunction with our research to find materials that could be used, led us to the construction of two large binders of materials, one of model articles and images from the growing number of books on rap and hip-hop culture, and the other from the array of youth magazines and newspaper articles that have emerged recently to give textual coverage to the various artists, images, issues, and events.

I duplicated both binders of information for the two focal teachers to have in the classrooms and also worked with them to choose particular texts from this accumulated material for specific uses in the intervention either as models of writing or as representations of themes. These materials were categorized and referenced in relationship to several themes that emerged, which we decided should be focal points in the curriculum. The themes were identity and self-definition; values and beliefs; issues surrounding language, style, and dress; the cultural characterizations of males and females and adults and youth; censorship and related themes of freedom, power, and voice; relationships (family, friends, male/female); violence and its causes and consequences; and roles and influences of the media in cultural production. These materials were in the forms of newspaper and magazine articles; short stories; visual materials like advertisements, pictures, and album covers; the written texts of songs along with audio materials like compact discs and cassettes; and some audiovisual materials. The point was to have far more materials available than actually needed in order to appeal to a wide range of individual student interests. We then found appropriate models in our materials that allowed us to demonstrate rhetorical correspondences to other texts of edited English and discussed and agreed on the instructional strategies to be used.

Ms. Parks and another focal teacher in Oakland were asked to keep their own written records of their observations of the progress of the intervention, to the extent possible, while two graduate student researchers working with the project observed the classes and collected qualitative data. Early responses by students were illuminating in a number of ways. Ms. Parks reported that as soon as she brought the binders of articles and materials into her class, her students started going through them on their own before the intervention was scheduled to begin. They were very excited about the articles in the binders, and they were hardly able to wait to actually start reading, discussing, and writing about them in class.

Student responses on the questionnaire along with our research led us to a number of provocative sources for descriptions and critiques of issues in rap and hip-hop music and culture as well as youth culture generally. We found ourselves reading and subscribing to magazines like *Vibe,* and *The Source,* and *Details* as well as reading the many pieces of academic research (and some of the commercial research) that is attempting to understand the workings of this exploding and explosive phenomenon. It is becoming clear, however, that we were aiming at a moving and mutating target, but we knew from the research that any real understanding especially of urban teens requires understanding hip-hop culture, the largest sub-culture of urban teens.

Our teacher/researcher team had to necessarily operate within an ethnographic framework because in many cases the student/informants in our target classrooms knew much more about the artists and issues we were sourcing than we did as participant/observers. Fortunately, the two graduate student researchers were in their mid-twenties and were able serve as the bridge between the students and our teacher/researcher team. However, though students at varying levels were participants in hip-hop culture, they had not read extensively and thought deeply about many of the provocative issues that this culture both raises and represents. It was at this intersection that the viability of our project rested—between their interests and our providing information and class time that allowed them to extend their interests. This intersection, however, was also a place where the students' personal/cultural knowledge and interests could be brought together with our schooling goals that consisted of further developing their thinking and writing skills.

Two brief examples are drawn from our use of the interview by Alan Light of "the artist formerly known as Prince" in *Vibe* magazine and an article by Donnell Alexander in the *San Francisco Bay Guardian* on the "culture clash" between rappers and hip-hop journalists (Light, 1994; Alexander, 1994). The interview centered on the controversy caused when the man who used to be called Prince used the occasion of his thirty-fifth birthday to inform the world that he was changing his name to a symbol described as follows:

> [The symbol] in one form or another, has been part of his iconography in recent years. (After starting as a simple combination of the symbols for male and female, it sprouted another flourish when it became the title of his last album; he has also signed autographs with the symbol for some time.) . . . Warner Bros. sends out software allowing the new name to be printed, but jokes and frequent references to "Symbol Man," "the Glyph," and "What's-His-Symbol" start turning up in the press. (Light, 1994, p. 46)

In illuminating aspects of the internal dialogue that goes on inside hip-hop culture, the article centers on the controversy caused by increasing antagonisms between rappers and some of the journalists who write about their work, which occasionally results in physical confrontations. Alexander described the situation as follows:

> As hip-hop moves into its teenage years, relations between the primarily young, black, inner-city artists who make the music and the primarily young, black, college-educated journalists who write about it are more strained than ever. A combination of factors, including

> rap's increasing clout in the pop marketplace, a growing body of
> critical writing about the music, and pronounced class differences
> between writers and rappers, have created a dangerous new trend
> in hip-hop—rap artists physically threatening and sometimes even
> attacking journalists they feel have slighted them in print.
> (Alexander, 1994, pp. 39–40)

In discussions of these writings, students were able to understand, explore, and make connections between the issues in ways that mirrored strategies that we as educators would want to see employed in the rigorous explication of any academic or otherwise school-based text. The issues quite clearly are provocative in the way they focus on topics that would have a place in college courses on theories of literacy or on theories of literacy criticism. In the interviews, for example, it became immediately clear that one must take into consideration the functions of oral versus written language that are latent in an identity quest and that demand a de-coupling of our traditional associations between signs and sounds; consideration of these functions is as good a springboard as any for reinterrogating our fundamental understanding of how we make meaning and thus sense of the world.

The issue of identity and the realization of identity through language carried students down similarly fruitful intellectual paths. The article on the hip-hop controversy is just as densely packed with issues that focus on authorial intention, textual ownership, and intellectual property rights and responsibilities. Essentially, students were able to probe these issues in pieces that attracted or intersected with their interests enough to sustain their investigation beyond merely superficial readings. In the process, we were able to model the conventions of more appropriate readings that are used to operate on a variety of texts, including other school-based texts.

Patterns in student writings from the intervention are just beginning to emerge, but so far they support our contentions that there are rhetorical correspondences between popular cultural texts and other edited English texts and these texts can be used jointly as models for students, motivating students so that they learn to write and to become prolific producers as well as consumers of texts.

Conclusion

In becoming ethnographers of student experiences in hip-hop culture, the focal teachers and I were not only learning where some points of connection could be made for learning in schools, we were also learning a bit more about where points of connection could be made between youths and adults. As educators we ask students to study things we have seen to be important in our world, but our success with them also depends on our efforts to understand things they have deemed important in theirs. Businesses are certainly doing their homework as different marketing and consulting firms vie to be recognized as the primary authority on the hip-hop generation in order to "fully develop" a market of more than fifteen million young people in America alone. Our reason for doing our homework is decidedly different and decidedly more important. The kind of work we do can help keep cultural worlds from drifting so far apart that they become mutually incomprehensible.

This chapter began with the notion that in order to be effective for significantly more students, education has to foray beyond traditional structural and cultural borders and make inroads in curriculum and instruction that successfully comprehend diversity. Bay View High is a site that is working to create new avenues of teaching and learning that are broad enough for the cultural traffic between the school and the communities it serves to travel in both directions. The events and scenes from this school blend with the other studies presented in this book to illuminate some of the key problems and possibilities of transforming classroom discourse and culture. I deliberately drew on scenes and images from the documentary film on this school along with our research at this site because, despite obvious problems, it reflected back some of the most salient ways that official school culture and a variety of different cultures can both connect or miss possible connections. I also wanted to acknowledge that a popular culture source like a video documentary could be valuable as data in the same way as other more traditionally accepted sources. This acknowledgment is in line with one of the arguments of this book that the materials we source in building pedagogy and curriculum can and must come from additional sites of untapped cultural resources.

The perceptions of students, teachers, administrators, and parents on the system of tracking in the school offered prominent vantage points for looking at changing school culture. Voices were heard from both sides of the tracks, with claims being made on the one hand that de-tracking was now segregating students inside the classrooms and hurting the more skilled students, with others arguing that it was increasing the achievement, retention, and esteem of underachieving students. Our observations and analyses of classes that were not yet de-tracked showed that the tracking system was severely hurting those students who were placed in the lower track. The consequences of tracking, of traditional curricula and teaching techniques, or of some combination of the three were shown to be key contributors to the disaffection and apathy that many students exhibited.

I also argued that much of the disruptive behavior of students was another negative consequence that could be traced in some degree to one or more of these features that a number of teachers and administrators at the school were actively working to change. This was important because it meant that students of color—particularly those defined as "involuntary minorities"—rather than being perceived as having relatively fixed oppositional behavior in relation to school culture because of their historical position of "castelike" subordination, were seen as resistant to the debilitating nature of the pedagogy and curriculum to which they were being exposed. The data implied that students were not necessarily resistant to achieving per se because they assumed that efforts to achieve were futile and that the job-ceiling was low. The greater factor seemed to be the problem that the pedagogy and curriculum neither gained nor reflected their interests and needs and therefore did not motivate them to achieve. The disheartening consequences of structural problems like tracking along with pedagogical and curriculum problems were graphically revealed in classrooms where the same teacher taught in separate tracks. Yet de-tracking alone clearly is not enough. The challenges of effectively reaching students go far beyond that as evidenced by the way that some attitudes and behaviors of students in one of the college writing classes that I observed and described in Chapter 3 mirrored those of students in problematic classes described in this chapter. These situations affirm once again what we already know about the necessity for high teacher expectations and appropriate levels of challenge, but they also illustrate the importance of establishing a sense of community through classroom discourse and culture in order to optimize conditions for learning.

This chapter also detailed a variety of ways that some teachers successfully created challenging and affirming classroom activities and environments for learning. Their transformations of classroom discourse significantly changed both the locus of control and the proportions of teacher-versus-student talk in class. But these teachers did not just give over control to the students. Rather, they employed sophisticated communication strategies that required a comfort with and skill for spontaneity to get students meaningfully involved as contributors and even as leaders in the discussions. This is especially important in high schools where students need to master more complicated communication interactions consistent with their increasing age and maturity.

These effects would not be possible, however, if the teachers were not additionally sensitive to the complex issues of identity and culture that students struggle to express and that in other ways also gets revealed in classroom discourse. This sensitivity allowed teachers to build on what students already knew to give meaning to presentations of new knowledge. It allowed students, as one teacher aptly noted, "to really look within themselves and grow."

In conjunction with various active and integrative teaching technologies, these teaching perspectives were important aspects of a transformative pedagogy and curriculum that changed classroom experiences of "mediocre sameness" by making viable connections between streets and schools. Yet, the real success of all of these strategies depended on the social relationships that the teachers established with their students through a variety of relationship-building rituals. When these relationships were functioning such that classrooms also became communities of learners, a young teacher could look a towering male student in the eye (without experiencing fear or encountering anger) and demand that he give her the dice she discovered he had, then motivate him again to try shooting for excellence.

5 Reflecting Diversity in a Mutable Curriculum

"[T]he curriculum should be both a window and mirror for students, that they should be able to look into others' worlds, but also see the experiences of their own race, gender and class reflected in what they learn."

Emily Style, 1992

Like Bay View, the San Francisco Bay Area high school discussed in the previous chapter, Grand Crossing High School in Chicago was also a place of tremendous diversity. Its approximately 2,000 students reflected twenty-one ethnic groups, though four of those groups—African Americans, Asian Americans, Latino Americans, and European Americans—made up 80 percent of the student body, with each comprising about one-fifth of the school's total population. The additional fifth was a mixture of the other seventeen groups.

However, defining the students with broad ethnic designations was deceptive as became clear when students were asked to identify themselves. For example, one questionnaire that I administered to the two focal classes ended with a section requesting that the students identify themselves by age, sex, and ethnicity. For ethnicity, many responses were typified by one student who simply wrote "mixed." Other responses, beyond the more common labels, were: Black and Indian; Irish and Native American; Irish, German, and Apache Indian; Spanish and French; French and Italian; Assyrian/Arabic; Iranian; Serbian; Ecuadorian; Cuban; Filipino; and Lebanese [this student put in the qualifying statement that she was born in Beirut but had been raised in Chicago since she was eight]. Other students played with this question by making responses such as the following: "Hint—a Nubian Queen"; or, "For me to know and you to find out"; or, in one case, just a question mark. Despite the fact that there was some playing around, it was also clear that many students were grappling with the extremely complicated issue of identity. Several students responded simply with the word "American."

Actually, these were atypical demographics for a Chicago public high school. The racial and ethnic composition of most Chicago high schools is extensively homogeneous because of historical patterns of segregation. But Grand Crossing was located in an area that was going through significant change in the ethnicity of its residents. Additionally, many of the African American and Latino students were bused in from as far away as the opposite side of the city, with the trip requiring up to two hours each way. Consequently, Grand Crossing had become an unusually rich site for diversity.

Where the study at Bay View looked in part at a curriculum intervention that was based in popular culture, the study at Grand Crossing looked at ways that two focal teachers dealt with the issue of reflecting diversity in a traditional high school English curriculum. This one-year ethnographic study that was completed in 1993 included classroom observations of each teacher's two senior English classes (along with audiotaping or videotaping of specific classroom events like project presentations and play performances), teacher interviews, and student interviews and questionnaires. The requirement for senior English in this school was world literature, and I observed and assessed instruction on such traditionally taught texts as the *Epic of Gilgamesh, Antigone* by Sophocles, the *Gulistan* by Sa'di, *The Stranger* by Camus, and an assortment of other pieces of literature from the class text (*Adventures in World Literature,* edited by Applegate et al., 1970). *The Great Gatsby* was also required as a representative sample of American literature. My discussion in this chapter illustrates ways that this curriculum was made more mutable especially by one of the teachers through incorporating elements of youth culture and specific group culture to effectively link the diverse needs and interests of the students to the learning of these traditional texts.

A Typical School

Based on the extent of its diversity, Grand Crossing High was an atypical school for Chicago. However, with respect to some of the major issues urban schools face, Grand Crossing was a typical Chicago urban school. On the basis of national test scores, it regularly placed around eleventh or twelfth academically among the sixty or so high schools in the city, and during this study it was also going through the application process to become a Coalition of Essential Schools site. But it also had a host of problems with gang and drug activity, truancy, pregnancy, and high drop-out rates. For example, at the same time that the student newspaper was celebrating the school's first city championship in football on its front page, it was also announcing and depicting Grand Crossing's first use of metal detectors to search students coming into school.

The school administration's discipline strategy in response to the changing complexion of the school, could be characterized in part by the following memo from the principal that was put in the mailboxes of my two focal teachers and all the other homeroom teachers in the school:

> *Assembly Bulletin 1/17/92*
> This bulletin pertains not only to the special senior-junior assembly on Friday, January 24, 1992 but also to future assemblies. (1) After reading these 3 pages go over them with your division today 1/17. (2) Note, everyone is to have an assigned seat recorded on their ID back. (3) Discuss getting to the auditorium early, which may involve planning not to stop at a locker. (4) Discuss the 5 rules of proper assembly decorum. [elicit these] (5) Note to your division that you will be early and by your seat. (6) Stress quietness, attentiveness, backs against the chair, proper posture, both feet on the floor, hands folded in the lap. (7) Teachers are to be seated only if those in the area around them are properly behaving, otherwise the teachers should be up and around teaching those who do not have proper assembly manners. (If they do not know or disregard your supervision, then it is your job to impose sanctions so they learn the consequences of their actions.)

The student and teacher personas invoked by this Assembly Bulletin reflect the school administration's desire for absolute control over students and near-absolute control over teachers in terms of how they did their jobs. It reveals the extent to which the students are viewed as objects to be managed, and it simultaneously reveals something of what they are subjected to. Through its excessively strict rules and tactics of manipulation it seems to go beyond getting teacher and student compliance—to a desire for complete subjugation.

Despite the administration's desire for the school to become a Coalition of Essential Schools site, the vast majority of the teaching that I observed generally seemed quite consistent with the findings of John Goodlad's major study (1984) of high schools, discussed earlier in this book. Several of his key findings are relevant here: the vehicle for teaching and learning is the total group; the teacher is the pivotal figure in the group; the norms governing the group derive primarily from what is required to maintain the teacher's strategic role; and, the emotional tone of the classroom is flat, and the curriculum is sterile. Goodlad and his colleagues observe that the students (to their credit) were perhaps more involved in their studies than the circumstances in their classes seemed to warrant. Their implication for the state of American education from the students' perspective was that it was immensely boring. Other studies substantiate Goodlad's position. A study of high school students and dropouts in Brooklyn provided interesting insights from students' perspectives about why classes are boring. Edwin Farrell (1988) of the City College of New York trained a group of high school students to collect ethnographic data on their classes and their peers. Among other things, he instructed them to record examples of their most interesting and most boring classes. To his surprise, students seemed to distinguish interesting from boring classes on the basis of the process rather than the content of the teaching. They reported that one of their most boring classes was devoted to a discussion of youth problems. Clearly, the topic of discussion alone did not excite these students; rather, their interest is more linked to the style of teaching the topic. Students claimed to be most engaged when teachers used a variety of resources to teach a concept. They also had various strategies for escaping the boredom like hiding out in the restrooms or cutting classes and riding the subways. Farrell concluded that for these students boredom became a kind of internal dropping out.

Goodlad (1984) noted that the central contradiction of this situation in American schools was that teachers often verbalized the importance of students increasingly becoming independent learners, but the picture that emerged from his data was one of student conformity and low to no initiative. Instead, what many teachers really seemed to value, if judged by their teaching strategies, was control. Or in the vivid words of one high school student, "We're birds in a cage. The door is open, but there's a cat just outside" (p. 109).

A Tale of Two Teachers

I will call the two focal teachers Ms. Cato and Ms. Stone. Ms. Stone was white, and Ms. Cato was Filipina. Both began teaching at Grand Crossing at the same time, about three years before this study began and not long after they had graduated from college. They both had taught senior English for at least two years before participating in this study. Single and in their mid-twenties during the year of this study, they were also friends who "hung out" together in school and occasionally outside of school. They usually ate lunch together each day in the teacher's lunchroom and often had extended discussions on everything from items in the news, to books and movies, to events in their personal lives.

Both teachers read voraciously, and would sometimes recommend books to each other to read jointly and discuss over lunch. While there, I read and participated in their discussions on the book of the moment, *Damage* by Josephine Hart (1991). Much was made of Hart's fluid but unsettling, two-page, first chapter in which her main character, "an efficient dissembler," presented both the urgency and uncertainty of the search for "an internal landscape" of identity and self-knowledge. Of interest was the fact that at times in some of their discussions, these teachers were confronting issues of identity and purpose in their own lives as teachers, as women, and as future mothers and spouses who were just a few years removed from the identity quests of their senior high school students.

Their similarities lessened, however, when it came to their ideas about and approaches to the construction and implementation of their curricula despite the fact that they were largely required to teach the same texts over the course of the school year. In every unit of instruction, Ms. Cato created entry points into the texts and the discussions, attempting to draw on student knowledge and interests as she perceived them. She often used popular cultural references or a specific group's cultural references to amplify and extend the thematic points of the text into familiar areas of her students' lives. Ms. Stone, on the other hand, took more of a school text-based approach to instruction. Yet, partially as a result of an early interest in and the influence of the Coalition of Essential Schools and also as a result of her discussions with Ms. Cato, Ms. Stone, too, questioned some of the traditional pedagogical practices that had been pretty much the accepted norm in this school. A special project she designed for her students during her teaching of *The Great Gatsby*, was one example of her attempts to blend more of their prior knowledge, interests, and experiences into the curriculum, and it was quite instructive to observe her pedagogy while she herself was in a process of critical transition in her approach to teaching.

The Great Gatsby

In Ms. Stone's classroom, the walls were filled with projects on the 1920s that students had completed while reading *The Great Gatsby*. The majority of students in Ms. Stone's classes mentioned *The Great Gatsby* as the work they enjoyed most or learned the most from in English during the school year. One student told how she liked the book because "it explains about the 1920s and about human nature. I learned that there are some people in this world that will die for love." The comments also revealed that it was greatly due to their work on the special projects about the era—connected by Ms. Stone to the unit on *Gatsby*—that this book was so memorable. Another student summarized how many students felt when she said, "I enjoyed doing the project on the 1920s. We had the option to work with other people which was fun. Till then the work on the story hadn't been interesting to me at all."

The project had a number of features that got students excited about learning, for example the opportunity to work with other students. The importance of this option was made dramatically clear when one female student said, "I can't express my ideas in class because I feel nervous talking in front of other people. I'm afraid I will answer the question wrong or something like that. I like working in groups though. I liked how we got into groups and how we shared our ideas on the subject." This fear of answering a question wrong in teacher-directed discussions was echoed by many students. As one young man noted, "I'm afraid I might answer some question the wrong way and make a fool out of myself." Interestingly, the project's presentation requirement did not cause as much anxiety about speaking before the group partially because students were presenting on what they knew rather than potentially revealing what they didn't know. Also, because students felt they were having fun, they were more relaxed even about their mistakes, as the following student indicated. "The project she gave was pretty fun. I got up in front of the class and made a fool of myself. It was fun though."

Ms. Stone had taught *Gatsby* twice before, but this was her first year of doing this type of project in conjunction with the book. Ms. Stone said that students' positive response actually surprised her. "I thought that they would be saying, oh, I don't want to do this; we don't want to do this. But I found that a lot of them really got into it. I found that a lot of them were really creative people, and that a lot of them really had a good time with it."

Ms. Stone went on to describe how she had imagined the project:

> I thought for them to really understand what Fitzgerald was trying to get across in the novel, because it's such a statement on society in the 1920s, that they would have to know what was going on in society in the twenties. . . . I saw this project as a way to both introduce them to the twenties and to see how far they were along in terms of being able to do independent research. I had them select a topic on something that happened in the twenties or how things were in the twenties. I gave them a lot of suggestions. I covered how the Apollo theater was formed at that time. About the jazz age. I talked about how they could do their projects on fashion or on dance. . . . So I spent a period giving them many ideas. You know, if they were into boxing, who was good at boxing at that time? You know, Babe Ruth in baseball and things like that. And I made them select something.
>
> The culmination of the project was in some form of presentation, and some of them did homemade movies. Some of them did a radio broadcast that could have occurred during that time, including props for the kind of noises that would have been heard during those old radio shows. And I had one girl—this was fascinating—she wrote a computer program that allowed her to depict the fashions. She projected the computer images through the overhead onto the screen to show what the fashions looked like on the wall. I got a lot of poster boards too. Some took the easy way out. Many of them brought in music, brought in props, got other people involved, got their classmates involved. I told them that I wanted them to do their projects individually, but if they wanted to work in groups of two or three that they could, but the work had to be enough to justify more than one person's involvement.

Upon reflection Ms. Stone also saw that while doing the projects, her students had found ways to relate to the issues and themes in the novel or to take ownership of the period in terms of their own background and culture even though many of them did not see themselves portrayed physically or positively in the work. The novel's thematic focus was not negated, but amplified by being used as a springboard into explorations of Ellis Island, the trade unions, class struggle, the Ku Klux Klan, jazz, the Apollo Theater, the 1919 Riots, World War I, etc. In so doing, a broader, multicultural interest was served as the individual projects allowed the curriculum to work as a mirror as well as a window. Each student was allowed a variety of access points to the novel's central themes based on the individual's unique backgrounds and interests, and they gained in-depth understandings of these themes through their project presentations. As a student in her class aptly noted, "we presented aloud, understanding one another, having respect and expressing our feelings. . . . You really don't exactly und—*initiate-response-evaluate*—erstand at first, but as you listen to them, you start to comprehend on things they say."

Despite the success of her incursion into an alternative approach with *The Great Gatsby*—which gave her insights into the strengths and creativity of her students that were not revealed through her previous approach—Ms. Stone's overall teaching strategies revolved around lectures and texts on the curriculum materials and an initiation -response-evaluation (IRE) form of discussion. In line with the school administration's tough stance, Ms. Stone prided herself on being strict and keeping order in her classes. She felt this was necessary in part because these students were seniors, but also because they came from such diverse home and community backgrounds. In other words, she saw the diversity as potentially explosive. In talking about her strategies for getting students involved in doing the work Ms. Stone stated, "Because they are seniors, duress is very effective. Because they could fail and then won't graduate, I have to threaten them, and I have to stand behind what I say. . . . I give kids chances, but I have my limits."

A look at one of Ms. Stone's class discussions on *The Great Gatsby* reveals how elements of tradition and reform exist simultaneously in the same teacher, in the same classroom, in the same school. Her desk, at which or upon which Ms. Stone invariably sat while leading discussions, was centered in the front of the classroom. Above the chalkboard behind her desk was the following sign, which could be read from anywhere in the room:

CLASSROOM RULES
1. The teacher is always right.
2. When the teacher is wrong, refer to Rule 1.

Ms. Stone started the class by saying, "If you think I was strict on the project, you haven't seen strict yet. I want top-drawer quality [on our next assignment]." She explained the next assignment and then announced that the discussion that day would be on *The Great Gatsby*. As class progressed, all the students had their books open and were reading along in the text. However, only two or three students were raising their hands and attempting to answer her questions. Mark and Margaret were two of these more vocal students. Ms. Stone's questions led the students; she tried to get them to come up with specific answers; said "right" or "no" to their responses; and, sometimes answered her own questions. For the most part, the discussion was a retelling of the story. It drew to a close with the following bit of dialogue surrounding the accident scene where Myrtle Wilson was killed:

> *Ms. Stone:* Any questions?
>
> *Margaret:* Why did Tom say that Gatsby's car wasn't his?
>
> *Ms. Stone:* Good question. Why did Tom say to George Wilson that Gatsby's car wasn't his own?
>
> *Mark:* Maybe he wanted to set him up or something.
>
> *Ms. Stone:* Set him up for what? In a way your statement, yeah but I don't no if you're meaning it how I'm perceiving it.
>
> *Mark:* Yeah, set . . . set him up. Uh, frame him.
>
> *Ms. Stone:* No. You guys have seen too many, too many uh . . .
>
> *Mark:* What's wrong with that?
>
> *Ms. Stone:* Too many movies lately, OK . . .
>
> *Mark:* That's a movie too. [The class had watched parts of the Robert Redford/Mia Farrow movie version of *Gatsby*.]
>
> *Ms. Stone:* Too many intricately plotted movies of the 1992 version like *Basic Instinct* and things. No. You guys, whenever you're going to argue something in literature you're going to have to go to the source itself to be able to back it up. It's, it's not a set up. It couldn't be a set up.

Actually, at this point in the story, Tom was indeed attempting to set Gatsby up. But this dialogue also focused Ms. Stone's attitude about popular culture—in this case, movies—in relation to literature and what count as valid references for explication. This attitude, which comes through in her teaching of the text itself, was in contradiction to the motive for doing the projects. It was further revealed in her closing remarks for that class:

> *Ms. Stone:* The way that Gatsby ends up is the only way that Gatsby could end up. That dream was not going to die. Gatsby was going to have to die before that dream would. It's his fatal flaw; it's what

kills him. It's like Macbeth. How many of you have read *Macbeth*? . . . OK, what was Macbeth's fatal flaw?

Margaret: Uh, greed?

Ms. Stone: Greed. His greed. Other people have argued other things or additional things like things about Lady Macbeth etc., but it was his greed. . . . Well, the fatal flaw that Gatsby has is his belief in his dream; his belief that he can go back to the past.

Ms. Stone had the following comments about class that day: "They were kind of dead today. . . . They were more like how they are on Monday. They're an OK group. They don't want to be here, they're seniors . . . . And some of them are probably not real happy with me because I'm making them do projects. . . . They know that on some things I am pretty cut and dry. I mean I've told them that if you do your work you will pass, if you don't do your work then you'll fail."

In this discussion on *The Great Gatsby*, Ms. Stone's students were in what I term a "literature loop." The main way that they were allowed to validate or extend their understandings of the literature under discussion was through references to other canonical texts. Despite the work on the projects, when it came to addressing the text directly, students' own experiences and personal references were not counted or developed as valid points of access.

This aspect of Ms. Stone's teaching contrasted with the approach used by the other focal teacher, Ms. Cato. Her strategies for teaching her entire curriculum included referencing the literature as much as possible with familiar experiences in the students' lives. "When you're seventeen," Ms. Cato said on the topic of teaching Fitzgerald's book, "who really cares that what happened in *Gatsby* is similar to what happened in some Shakespearean play. Who cares? I mean you get this question all the time. 'Why do we have to read this'? And if you're going to say because this is similar to what happened in some play or whatever, you know; the kids are not going to tune into that. . . . If you don't relate it to them, and show the meaning in it for them, then they automatically are going to tune you out."

Recalling her teaching of *The Great Gatsby*, Ms. Cato described a high point. It was the time when one of her students brought in a copy of *Sassy*, a magazine geared toward female teen interests, which had a fashion photo-essay entitled "Gatsby." In the middle of the class, she changed her lesson for the day to allow the students to explore the photo images and to try to relate them to the novel:

"It was not a perfect fit," Ms. Cato noted. "There were six or seven full-page photos with different combinations of two female models and one male model all in these absolutely gorgeous outdoor scenes and, you know, dressed in contemporary versions of twenties fashions. But the photos and captions seemed unclear in terms of the actual events in the book. So, we tried to figure out which model was supposed to be Daisy and which was supposed to be Jordan. We tried to figure out how we could tell. Like did one look more athletic in terms of her build, her clothes? Jordan was a pro golfer you know. And who was the male model supposed to represent? Gatsby, Nick, Tom? How could we know based on how what was shown in the photos related to facts from the book? Were the captions helpful, or misleading? Well, we decided they were misleading and told there own little theme."

"One picture had the man and one of the women in a row boat. Was this supposed to be Gatsby and Daisy, or Nick and Jordan? We didn't remember any scene like this in the book. One student remembered that Daisy tried to be a matchmaker for Nick and Jordan and joked about putting them in a boat and pushing them out to sea. This made us decide we were supposed to take the couple in the boat for Nick and Jordan though a scene like that wasn't in the book. We tried to see if there was anything in the photos that gave away the fact that they were not really taken in the twenties. People thought the bicycle the girls were riding on looked too modern. One model had a watch on that looked too modern. In most cases we couldn't prove anything for sure, but they had to use their knowledge of the book and their knowledge of the period and some logic of their own, and it ended up being one of our best discussions."

The students in Ms. Cato's class seemed both relaxed and eager. Sometimes they raised their hands to talk, but most of the time they just spoke out. There was lots of laughter and some joking and signifying. Sometimes, during class, I would see a student take out a newspaper or another distraction, but then put it away after a couple of minutes. Nearly every class would get the students actively engaged. As one student put it, "Everyone almost participates, but if they don't, they sit there and listen and they don't criticize anyone. So, it's really easy to participate."

Ms. Cato's students really liked her classes, and they had definite reasons for why they did. What they mentioned most often was their feelings about the way she taught. They echoed the sentiments of students in Farrell's study (mentioned above) regarding the value of a variety of learning resources. One said, "[She] adds some variety to her teaching technique, you never know what she's going to do next. Sometimes she brought munchies for us, and she seems so happy everyday that it rubs off on everybody." Another student noted, "I got off some stress in the class because of how the teacher teaches." A third said, "The teacher makes it fun and interesting while learning at the same time. I hate boring classes." A fourth student added, "I like her style. She has a unique way of teaching. It's not boring like other teachers because we do a lot of different things. Another example of the many student comments like these was, "Our teacher always finds a way to make everything in our book more interesting . . . the way we did the play, the learning games. We are all a team, and we help each other at anytime." Additionally, one student reflected the feelings of many when she said, "We talk about different things that relate to our daily lives. She shows us in a practical way what our stories and plays are all about."

It was revealing also that when Ms. Cato's students were asked which piece of literature they enjoyed the most, they cited a range of literature from the ancient to the contemporary, which supported the point that the style of teaching was what made the content accessible. As one of her students responded, "I really can't say I liked one thing best because I've enjoyed everything we've read." Some, however, noted that they liked selections from the ancient works such as *Gilgamesh,* and *The Gulistan* while others indicated they most enjoyed novels such as *The Stranger* and *The Great Gatsby.* Also, there was consistent mention of their work with the play, *Antigone.* In the words of one student, "It was very interesting. It was set back centuries ago, but I was still able to relate it to today's times. It taught us what is right to do in your heart."

Antigone

After Ms. Cato had finished teaching *Antigone,* I asked her how she felt that unit of instruction went. Her self-critique, which follows, was also an accurate reflection of my observations.

> I thought the *Antigone* trial was an especially good experience in terms of the things we did with the play. First of all, I let them decide the whole process . . . I let them decide on what they wanted to do, and when they brought up the suggestion to put Antigone on trial, I personally thought it was a bad idea. I didn't think it would be . . . you know, she's definitely guilty, so why bother trying her. But really what happened, what came out of it was that the students that they picked to prosecute and defend Antigone came up with some really good questions that blew my mind, and that I didn't even think of. Just because of that, I thought it was something that was enjoyable. And then you could see the kids when they were watching this whole thing. During the trial, when this series of questions was coming out, you could see that their minds were already jumping ahead and that they could see where these questions were leading and they were thinking of things they hadn't thought of before. They were learning, and I was learning at the same time.
>
> And I think from looking at the expressions on the kids' faces, that they were surprised that someone who was their peer could think of things like this, and that the teacher hasn't even thought along these lines; that during when we were reading *Antigone,* I didn't ask some of the questions that the kids did. They were surprised that some of their peers could think of these things, or draw

some conclusions or come up with new perspectives that even the book or the teacher hasn't thought of.

I think what they got out of it was that it was applicable to them and that it was a moral discussion or a philosophical discussion of issues rather than concrete details about when *Antigone* was written, that *Antigone* was a part of a cycle of three plays, blah, blah, blah. I think they got things out of the play that you can't measure. This came through when I asked them to write up one man-made law that goes against their personal code of ethics. But we also have contests between classes on *Antigone* to review the content, and to go over things that did have a specific answer.

These strategies did enhance the students' understanding of the play. As one student noted, "We got in a circle and read it aloud, and after that we had a trial that gave us a better view of the story."

One of Ms. Cato's contests had her two senior classes compete with each other to do the best condensed or summary rendition of the play. Again, her students were encouraged to make the decisions about what they would focus on in their renditions, but they had to be able to defend why each one reflected something elementally significant about the play. Both classes worked extremely hard on their renditions for about a week of classes creating their scenes, making props and costumes, and practicing. On the appointed day, the two classes met together and presented their renditions to each other.

One class presented a modernized condensed rendition of key scenes from the play and began with Creon, who was cast as a gay king, calling a press conference to give a kind of "State of the Union" address. The African American male who played Creon was superb and the calculated deconstruction of the images of manhood, leadership, and power was a masterful twist that was not lost on the student audience. The "independent" panel of students whose job was to determine the winner of the competition voted this rendition to be the best. But the other rendition was just about as good. In that version, students used musical selections to anchor each theme, beginning with a '70s standard, "War: What Is It Good For," as background for the fighting going on in Thebes, and including songs like "Money, Money, Money" by another '70s rhythm-and-blues group for the pivotal scene where Creon accuses Tiresias of being a prophet who is trying to profit by his wisdom. The two renditions were fun and at times funny, but they also revealed incisive understandings of complex themes in *Antigone*.

The Gulistan and Gilgamesh

Though Ms. Cato always worked to make connections between the texts and her students' lives, sometimes these connections happened serendipitously through the texts themselves. Her teaching of *The Gulistan* is an example of the former, while her teaching of *Gilgamesh* an example of the latter. *The Gulistan,* a collection of stories that are both didactic and entertaining, was written by Sa'di (born around 1200). In teaching one of the stories, "The Manners of Kings," Ms. Cato had the students compare its thematic point about truth to a popular song titled "The Policy of Truth" by Depeche Mode. The story had raised a provocative point about the possible misuse of even truthful statements.

> The king being displeased with these words, said: "That lie was more acceptable to me than this truth thou hast uttered because the former proceeded from a conciliatory disposition and the latter from malignity; and wise men have said: A falsehood resulting in conciliation is better than a truth producing trouble." (*The Gulistan,* 1970 ed.)

The words from "The Policy of Truth" which Ms. Cato had provided on a handout were also ambiguous about the ultimate value of truth. "Now you're standing there tongue tied/You'd better learn your lesson well/ Hide what you have to hide/And tell what you have to tell" (Depeche Mode, 1989).

After reading the one-page story and then playing the Depeche Mode song, Ms. Cato asked the class, "Do you think society places more value on the truth? Are there good reasons to tell lies?" The ensuing discussion was animated by lots of laughter and total class involvement. A student asked Ms. Cato to state her belief on the difficult choices regarding lying versus telling the truth which had been raised in the discussion. Ms. Cato gave her own opinion, but it was clear that her opinion was one that went alongside those presented by her students and that it was not the definitive one simply because she was teacher. "For homework," Ms. Cato said as the discussion came to a close, "I want you to tell the whole truth, and the absolute truth for a whole day, and see how many times you are tempted to lie, or see what difficulties you get into in telling the truth. Then write me a short essay, at least two pages, about your experiences with the truth." After the class, Ms. Cato told me that Depeche Mode had another song that made specific reference to the pivotal scene in *The Stranger* where the Arab is shot, and that she uses this song, too, with similar success when she teaches that text.

Sometimes the text being studied naturally lent itself to brief or simple ritual-like performances, as in the story of *Gilgamesh.* The repetition and rhythm of this written transformation of an oral story was made more interesting to Ms. Cato's students when she structured appropriate parts of the reading into call-and-response formats that gave them more of a sense of how this story might have originally been told. This and other techniques of drawing on correspondences to and competencies in features of African American or youth discourse made this story come alive for her students. For example, Gilgamesh used a bragging/boasting discourse style when he encountered Siduri (the woman of the vine, the maker of wine) in an attempt to persuade her to let him in to her garden and to help him find the secret of everlasting life.

> Young woman, maker of wine, why do you bolt your door; what did you see to make you bar your gate? I will break in your door and burst in your gate, for I am Gilgamesh who seized and killed the Bull of Heaven, I killed the watchman of the cedar forest, I overthrew Humbaba who lived in the forest, and I killed the lions in the passes of the mountain. (*The Epic of Gilgamesh*, 1970 ed.)

Students were excited to see this bragging/boasting style with which many were familiar represented in a "school work" text. They were able to connect it to the sports discourse of "greats" like Muhammad Ali who boasted of "floating like a butterfly and stinging like a bee." It also helped them to more clearly see and understand the larger-than-life proportions of this ancient "hero," Gilgamesh.

There were other lessons, too, in which Ms. Cato used simple, ritual-like structures as part of her approach to learning the texts. One example was when she broke up the class into groups of seven and had each student in a group learn two lines of a Shakespearean sonnet that had either been assigned by the teacher or collectively chosen by the group. The idea was for each student to say his or her two lines with appropriate expressiveness and in the right order to create a collaborative oral rendition of the sonnet. The students seemed to enjoy working together to memorize and orchestrate their sonnets, learning and entertaining themselves in their groups, as well as eventually performing them as groups for each other. The same groupings were also used for discussion and analysis to explore the complex meanings of the sonnets. At the end of these activities, most group members had memorized the entire group sonnet. In addition, students often demonstrated intricate understanding of their sonnets' themes and images as well as significant understanding of the various sonnets that were prepared and performed by the other class groups.

Ms. Cato's success in teaching her students was not merely a consequence of the strategies she used to build on student interest and competencies. She genuinely cared about her students' lives as well as their learning and her students knew this. She also worked to construct an overall class culture that made students comfortable talking in class and willing to takes risks in presenting their ideas. A key ingredient in the culture of her class was constant praise by her for the students and also by the students for each other. As one student noted, "The teacher always points out a good aspect about something you share with the class and this allows to get an insight on how you feel without being condemned."

Teaching to Diversity

Elements of a pedagogical model that comprehends diversity can be extrapolated from this study of Ms. Stone and Ms. Cato's classes. Though one must certainly consider the differing effects resulting from the teaching styles of the two teachers, it is more important to this analysis to look at points in their pedagogy when things were working well for their students—when students were highly motivated and actively engaged—to draw out implications for teaching and learning. In line with the earlier noted point made by Tharp and Gallimore (1988), it is significant to look at teachers' actual practices to assess how teachers should conduct themselves in classrooms to be more effective. Also, in conjunction with the point noted earlier by Ellsworth (1995), it is important to understand how these teaching practices as well as the curricula themselves work as acts of representation that can either reflect or deny the images and interests of students. Too often as Sleeter and Grant (1991) have earlier noted, the textbooks at the center of school curricula present a highly selective and static view of knowledge and social reality thereby reinforcing only the dominant images and interests in society, which students are encouraged to accept rather than question.

What Ms. Stone was able to do through her students' projects specifically and what Ms. Cato was able to do through her teaching generally was to circumvent the limitations of a textbook and a canonical, text-based curriculum with strategies that overcame some of the inherent cultural and linguistic biases. This was done by extending classroom learning to major areas of concern and interest for their students. As a student in Ms. Cato's class said, "We always had open discussions; we could talk about anything happening around us and what it has to do with English." When students were allowed to link the themes of their class texts to investigations of issues and topics that were important to them and that were related to their own experiences, they learned to "re-present" themselves through teacher guided discoveries of their own unique voices.

When the curriculum was made more mutable, both teachers were at times surprised at what students could contribute to the explication of important issues and topics. Recall Ms. Cato's point about the trial of Antigone where her students came up with things that "blew [her] mind," or Ms. Stone's reflections on the complex and intriguing projects that her students were able to create. In both cases the structure of classroom activities provided considerable flexibility and room for student voices and choices. As Ms. Cato said of the trial, "I let them decide the whole process." Ms. Stone similarly had spent a lot of time helping students consider a variety of possible approaches to their projects. These strategies allowed their students to take ownership of the respective periods and themes in the novels and plays even when they could not initially see themselves represented physically or positively in these works.

Examples of student engagement is evident in several of the projects created by African American and other students on topics such as the Jazz Age, the Apollo Theater, and the Harlem Renaissance. The time frame of *The Great Gatsby* is also an important period in American history for African Americans, and though it was not Fitzgerald's purpose in the novel to tell their story, he does hint at racial issues and tensions of the times. Clearly, Tom Buchanan was meant to be viewed as a pathetic racist with his pseudoscientific pronouncements about the dangers of the white race being utterly submerged and his fearful contemplation of the breach of "the last barrier of civilization"—intermarriage between blacks and whites. But even Nick, the narrator whose moral character was more evolved, referred to the "three modish negroes" in a limousine, driven by a white chauffeur, which passed them on the way to New York as "two bucks and a girl." The point that Nick gleaned in wonderment at this sight was that "Anything can happen . . . 'anything at all.'" There were only four glimpses of blacks in the entire novel, yet in each case their depiction was used to define or accentuate a key aspect of a major character or a pivotal scene.

Essentially, what Fitzgerald relies on in his skeletal portrayal of blacks is what Toni Morrison (1992) has termed "metaphorical shortcuts." In *Playing in the Dark,* she explores how metaphorical shortcuts work both consciously and unconsciously to configure, camouflage, and marginalize black presence in American literature. Henry Louis Gates Jr. (1988) notes that a major contribution of the Black Arts Movement of the sixties and seventies was to begin to change the absence signified by blackness in the Western tradition to a signified presence. The dismissive "othering" of people and language is revealed in what Morrison calls American Africanism—"a nonwhite, Africanlike (or Africanist) presence or persona . . . the denotative and connotative blackness that African peoples have come to signify, as well as the entire range of views, assumptions, readings, and misreadings that accompany Eurocentric learning about these people" (p. 6). Morrison's analysis of this process of dismissive othering illuminates ways that literary "blackness" and "whiteness" are produced in texts as well as the effects of their production.

Through their projects on jazz, the Apollo Theater, the 1919 Riots, World War I, Ellis Island, trade unions, class struggle, even the Ku Klux Klan, Ms. Stone's students were able to 'click' on the flat icons of blackness or otherness that Fitzgerald had screened and open a window into a fuller, richer representation of images and issues of that period. In so doing they were also integrating their learning of literature with history, geography, art, music, politics, and media. The projects allowed them to move from the novel's text to its larger context and to see and question some of the selective views that were operating as subtexts, thereby enlarging their understanding of social reality. A similar questioning of perceptions of social reality was evident in Ms. Cato's classes' rendition of scenes from *Antigone* with Creon cast as a gay king. Through performance activities like the rock musical scenario of the play as well as activities like a courtroom dramatization of the play, students were able to build their understanding and analysis of this canonical text within cultural frames more directly situated in familiar kinds of sociocultural experiences.

Ms. Cato felt that critical learning was taking place in her students. As she said, "You could see their minds were already jumping ahead . . . and they were thinking of things they hadn't thought of before. They were learning, and I was learning at the same time." These instances of students teaching each other as well as teachers learning from their students represents one of the ways that voice and equality are connected. As students became authoritative about topics through taking more responsibility for their learning, their voices also gained authority. There were times when Ms. Cato would give her own opinions on the topics under discussion, but because the strategies used to access the topics had helped students clarify their own voices, Ms. Cato's opinion was not necessarily the definitive one simply because she was the teacher.

Another way that voice and equality connected was in the respect and appreciation engendered for the array of voices that were able to be heard. Though Ms. Stone did initially see her class's diversity as potentially explosive, her change during the projects to more student-focused, student-centered classroom talk actually increased the sense of community by revealing the quality as well as the similarities of student perceptions, even amid differences. One of Ms. Stone's students expressed this best when she explained how presenting "aloud" had helped students to better understand and respect each other. When an Asian student in her class presented a controversial project on the KKK, Ms. Stone herself was surprised (and relieved) by the mature way that her students engaged the discussion and critique of this subject and their acceptance of the right of each student to have his or her point of view represented.

One of the most effective strategies that Ms. Cato used to open up the discussion and to allow for diverse points of view was her questioning technique. As she noted, "I don't think you ask them questions that have definitive answers because once, you know, you've taught them how to find answers, I mean as seniors, they can find factual answers for themselves." Not focusing on definitive answers helped to open up the discussion. As one young woman enthusiastically said, "I'm comfortable discussing in class because the teacher makes you want to talk. She does it by asking question after question that makes you really think. I love answering her questions."

The nature of classroom discourse in Ms. Cato's classes was a transformation of the initiation-response-evaluation (IRE) formula. As noted earlier, students sometimes raised their hands to be recognized before entering the discussion, but most of the time they just spoke out to the teacher and to one another in ways that required them as a group to manage a more internal locus of control consistent with a style that Kochman defined as receiver-centered. Students initiated more talk and took more turns to talk as the direction and control of talk was restructured to include significantly more discourse among students.

Ms. Cato, in fact, was implementing a coaching style of teaching that, like the coaches in the community sports program, centered on the speaking rights and performances of the students as key components in their development. She was not aware of the work of scholars like Bakhtin, but her reflective and intuitive transformation of the curriculum to facilitate the play and amplification of diverse student voices effectively linked elements of their primary speech genres to the text-based secondary speech genres of school. In the words of Bakhtin (1986), "the transfer of style from one genre to another . . . violates or renews the given genre" (p. 66). Through her methods for developing the "speaking consciousness" of her students, Ms. Cato was acting as an agent of transfer by sourcing and reworking the cultural material of her students' lives in order to renew life and learning in school.

The projects, plays, contests, and other activities in Ms. Stone and Ms. Cato's classes required collaborative and interpretive classroom activities that culminated in a variety of presentations and/or performances of student learning. These activities were dynamic intersections of knowledge acquisition and expression. They reflected alternatives to a traditional orientation toward the mastery of information as static and compartmentalized in distinct and rigidly defined disciplines. As Robert Reich (1991) notes, "Instead of emphasizing the transmission of information, the focus is on judgment and interpretation. . . . The student learns to examine reality from many angles, in different lights, and thus to visualize new possibilities and choices" (p. 232).

Concerns that students had of not wanting to appear foolish in front of their peers were mitigated by the authority and confidence they had gained from being given choices on what to present and of being able to build on their own experiences and interests. In some cases they had to convince other students to get involved on a project of choice. Negotiating among themselves to decide how to present a scene from *Antigone* or choosing to research and present an "authentic" radio broadcast from the twenties made the eventual presentation of their work part of a more authentic learning experience. They were presenting on what they knew, rather than being exposed for what they didn't know. Also, sharing and exchanging their ideas in groups had the effect of giving them trial runs on the substance of their presentations before they went before the class in general. In the nation's most effective schools, Reich points out that "[s]tudents learn to articulate, clarify and then restate for one another how they identify and find answers. They learn how to seek and accept criticism from peers, solicit help, and give credit to others. They also learn to negotiate—to explain their own needs, to discern what others need and view things from others' perspectives, and to discover mutually beneficial resolutions. These ideas are preparation for lifetimes of symbolic-analytic teamwork" (p. 233).

Since these projects and active performances offered students a variety of ways to exhibit both the breadth and depth of their learning, they often could not be evaluated in rigid, mechanical ways. Ms. Cato and Ms. Stone were aware of the need for more sensitive evaluation methods, but during the time of the study neither teacher felt she had developed a significantly new way of assessing her students' work. Both teachers, however, understood that their students learned things through these strategies that couldn't be measured or evaluated, such as ethical considerations and reflections on personal codes of behavior. They additionally agreed that some of the very students who seemed unmotivated by school in general would come alive and shine in collaborative work with other students and in various kinds of class projects and presentations. However, one area where Ms. Stone and Ms. Cato differed was in active learning strategies that involved student competition.

Ms. Stone consciously avoided competitive activities in her class, while Ms. Cato often consciously incorporated elements of competition into her learning activities. In fact, she felt that sometimes it was the competitive aspects of her lessons that elicited active participation. She had competitions between classes on the presentation of a scene from *Antigone*, using panels of student judges; she had contests to review specific content from the play; she used game formats for some of the quizzes; and the trial of Antigone itself was a competition between the lawyers for the prosecution and those for the defense.

I interviewed Ms. Cato's students extensively on their perceptions about their classes' competitive activities and found that, by and large, they liked the challenge these activities provided, the teamwork they required, and the excitement they engendered. The key seemed to be that the activities didn't focus so much on individual performances as they did on working in groups and teams, and though students didn't like to lose they seemed to keep in perspective that the ultimate object of the games was not to win but to learn. The learning games that Ms. Cato created actually operated as ordered, rule-governed systems, and the teamwork itself generated feelings of connectedness among students across some of the borders that can exist in diverse classrooms. Though competition was present, it was essentially competition between teams, and it often motivated more sophisticated levels of collaboration within teams as well as camaraderie and appreciation for the work of other teams. The students truly became players in the game of learning with Ms. Cato facilitating as a teacher/coach.

Conclusion

Ms. Stone and Ms. Cato's classes foreshadow the demographics of twenty-first century schools in terms of complexity and difference. One teacher was white, the other Filipina, but their ethnicities were not as important to this discussion as the fact that neither teacher could rely on her ethnic identification to enhance her success with her students. Rather, their efficacy depended more on ways that their specific instructional strategies motivated students to effectively engage the curriculum content. But being successful in motivating students to learn is difficult especially when their needs and interests are not homogeneous or unitary. Teachers not only have to develop curricula that build on students' backgrounds, perceptions, and interests, they have to do so in ways that provide a combination of intense challenge, excitement, and activity in learning at appropriate and accessible levels reflective of individual student needs. Ms. Stone and Ms. Cato's classes yielded insights into how aspects of youth popular culture as well as some aspects of African American culture could be utilized to facilitate the learning of traditional texts in school. There may be questions and concerns about particular elements of both teachers' practices. But from my observations and from the accounts of both teachers, the depth of learning engendered among their students and the extent of creativity unleashed was a direct result of the teachers acknowledging the students' choices and interests in accessing the curriculum content. The success of the results was surprising even to the teachers. By drawing on and valuing the raw materials of student experiences, these teachers were able to help their students refine and profit from them in numerous ways. According to Knapp with Adelman et al. (1995) in *Teaching for Meaning in High-Poverty Classrooms*, students should not only be actively and holistically engaged in making sense of their experience in school, they should also find meaning by connecting new learning experiences to their existing body of knowledge, assumptions, and meanings, much of which is rooted in their upbringing and cultural roots. Underlying Knapp's point is James Gee's notion mentioned earlier in this book that intellectual life must ultimately be connected to and expanded from the various cultural models that pattern experiences and perceptions.

In these teachers' attempts to understand, honor, and ultimately build on their students' experiences, they intentionally and in some cases inadvertently transformed the curriculum to allow for numerous points of entry. They experimented with novel ways to encourage their students to think, and they worked to create assignments that allowed students to reveal what they had learned in a variety of ways and in a variety of mediums such as homemade movies, radio broadcasts, computer displays, poster boards and other props, drawing on contemporary and provocative themes and images from popular culture. Ms. Stone was in the process of making her own critical transition to these perspectives, so these pedagogical and curricular strategies were seen much more pervasively in the teaching of Ms. Cato.

Ms. Cato used a coaching/mentoring style of teaching to create a classroom discourse and culture that was dialogical and receiver-centered and that accommodated her students' voices and choices in the content of the curriculum. In this sense she was also a teacher/ethnographer who drew on her students' varying sociocultural backgrounds and interests to better develop and ultimately expand the cultural models that patterned their perceptions. In the subjugating environment of the overall school, Ms. Cato saw herself as a change agent for her students by first motivating them to learn and then helping them to understand and challenge the constraints on their lives, both in and out of school. She took her students as well as herself seriously, and she set high expectations for the students' work. But she also used constant praise, publication, and performance of student works as tangible ways to make them feel their ideas were important and that their unique perspectives really mattered. These active learning strategies themselves created lots of fun and excitement in her classes, and by their own accounts her students were almost never bored. She employed a number of relationship-building rituals, and she found ways to blend aspects of academic talk with social talk. As one student noted, "We talk about different things that relate to our daily lives. She shows us in a practical way what our stories and plays are all about."

Finally, Ms. Cato's curriculum was always able to change to better serve a discovered interest or to allow for spontanteity. As one of her students noted, "[Y]ou never know what she's going to do next." This feature of her pedagogical style reflects the notion that learning can be more like a game. It is most highly stimulating when players are never quite sure what's going to happen next despite the fact that it is operating inside a rule-governed system. This orientation goes against too rigid an emphasis on specific lessons and unchanging learning objectives. It is an orientation toward a more mutable curriculum and a pedagogy for teaching it that I believe will be requisite to the style of learning needed in new century schools. When Ms. Cato spontaneously changed her lesson for the day to incorporate the photo essay on Gatsby into her discussion of the book, I came to see her approach to the curriculum more like the performance of a jazz composition in contrast to a classical music piece. She was the leader; she knew the melody; but there was room for improvisation and experimentation in the rhythms of learning being played in her class.

6 Imagining New Century Schools

The studies presented in earlier chapters focused primarily on teaching and learning in school settings that were characterized both by diversity and the need for strategies effective with underachieving students. These studies revealed a number of successful practices that have been employed in these settings and indicated how and why they worked for students. This final chapter synthesizes these practices into a model for teaching and learning and shows ways that this model addresses issues of schooling, especially secondary schooling, in the United States. I believe it has implications not only for educational settings like the ones described in the studies, but also generally for the challenges of teaching and learning in U. S. schools. Merely reforming educational practices in order to bring underachieving groups up to the levels of achieving groups generally ignores fundamental problems with U. S. education. It suggests that what we have to do is find ways to make underachieving students benefit from the educational process in the same way that achieving students do. This cycles us right into reproducing systems that may have worked to a degree before; but new global and technological exigencies, along with considerations of diversity, require better processes for teaching and learning for all learners.

Also, as I have argued earlier, the kind of learning needed for the next century is changing significantly. Instead of mastering information that is static and compartmentalized in distinct and rigidly defined disciplines, students need to be able to effectively integrate the learning of fundamental knowledges with other rapidly emerging and often transitory information and knowledge bases. They must be capable of both abstract and systematic thinking in order to discover, analyze, and make meaning of the patterns in processes that are changing even as they are being studied. They must develop skills for accessing and evaluating information from overwhelming quantities available from voluminous global sources, and they also must develop abilities to analyze, synthesize, and combine this information with fundamental knowledges in order to solve problems and create new knowledge.

In focusing on pedagogical strategies for facilitating integrated learning, it becomes paramount to restructure both the methods of communicating and the teaching of communication skills in the classroom. Moreover, new pedagogical strategies have to take into account the emergence of new communications technologies. These strategies will have to continue to improve ways of teaching reading, writing, speaking, and listening skills simultaneously and of using them in cross-curricular projects; but these strategies must also incorporate teaching and practicing skills for communicating in new mediums and intermodally among a variety of mediums as well as across cultures. These different modes of learning and interacting in classrooms are becoming requisites to apprehending the rapid, novel changes that are increasingly emblematic of U. S. and world cultures.

The following scenario of one classroom in one school projected about a decade into the future offers a model of teaching and learning that attempts to comprehend some of the challenges for new century schools. After presenting this scenario, I will connect implications and findings from the studies discussed in this book to particular features of the model to illustrate ways that a possible future is in process now.

Fast-Forward

At Bay View High, Ayni, a first-year student, felt a little nervous as she awaited her turn to present. It was getting toward the middle of the second hour of a Monday morning class on North American Studies, and Max was receiving polite applause for the presentation he was just finishing on the 1849 Gold Rush. Ayni, however, was not impressed. Max did have a knack for sound-graphic-text compositional techniques, but that should not mask substance, she thought. Anyone could go into the database of a PC-notebook and get the background information he used to situate the importance of this event. What bothered her was that some key considerations for understanding this period with respect to all the various groups involved were left out. Perhaps, because everyone looked ready for a break, most of the students didn't really challenge Max much in the response/critique segment.

Everyone still seemed fascinated by the technical capabilities of the new Pear 1's. These were the cool, new student PC-notebooks that replaced the bulky models everyone had used in junior high and which had weighed almost two pounds. New Pear 1's were being sold at a 25 percent discount in the school bookstore, and most first-year students had gotten their parents to purchase them one. Weighing in at exactly sixteen ounces, they were advertised as the "Pound of Knowledge." Mr. Clevelon always joked, however, that it was just a pound of information, and what people did with it would determine whether or not any knowledge happened. Ayni wasn't sure yet if she liked Mr. Clevelon; something about him reminded her of her father.

With this last image, Ayni's thoughts went in two directions. She put aside the father connection, however, and tried to figure out why she was still reserved toward Mr. Clevelon's teaching itself. He was certainly an excellent teacher and well liked by most of his students. He always received high mid- and end-of-year student evaluations, which everyone knew were key considerations in all teachers' salary and promotion decisions. In his career, he had twice won the students' Outstanding Teaching Award, and it was common knowledge that he would be running for a spot on the Language and Communication(s) Curriculum Committee at the end of the school year. He had also gained recognition for the success of his statewide Eight-Hour Novella Contest for high school students, modeled on the One-Day-Novel, World Cup Competition. He had worked out a foolproof electronic network for proctoring the whole contest simultaneously across the state. He said the contest challenged students to "write at the speed of thought."

A lot of students affectionately called Mr. Clevelon "Mr. C," and he had a large number of student mentees at all grade levels throughout the school, who called themselves the C-Corps. He had an especially dedicated following among the male and female extramural athletes. There were hardly any schools left that had P.E. classes, but Bay View, like most schools, had an extensive intramural sports and mind/body synthesis program that every student participated in for all four years. Each year, students chose one intramural sports team to be on and at least one class in yoga, dance, tai chi, shiatsu, and other alternatives from the mind/body class selections. But there were also extramural teams that competed with other schools, and Mr. Clevelon worked intensively with the students on these teams through the school's scholar/athlete program. The athletes he worked with saw themselves as a special subset of the C-Corps that they called the Warrior-Poets Society.

Mr. Clevelon, however, Ayni had resolved, tried to push too much of his students' learning through technology. Ayni knew this was just a question of emphasis, yet she had had other teachers who she felt kept technology in its place in school. For example, Ms. Cato, the teacher she had liked best so far, knew as much about computers as anybody, but her teaching always kept the interaction of her students with each other in the forefront of all class activities. Ayni remembered her experiences in Ms. Cato's class at Grand Crossing High where she had gone last year for three months as part of the National Junior High School Student Exchange Program, a new component of the high school National Student Exchange Program. Grand Crossing was one of about half the public schools in Chicago that had adopted 7–12 programs to connect junior high components to high schools. Ms. Cato had left teaching in the late nineties to pursue an acting career, but two years ago, after getting married and having a child, she had returned to teaching and apparently picked right up where she had left off, once again getting her students excited about learning. The personal dynamic that Ms. Cato brought to her teaching and the student dynamics that occurred in her classes were more important to Ayni than anything she ever found inside a PC-notebook.

Ayni had to admit, however, that there were times when the use of technology made things easier. For example, after open discussion and critique on presentations in Mr. Clevelon's class, each student also had to send comments to the presenters' private drop-boxes in the classroom electronic interchange network. She wanted to tell Max that his presentation had taken a nice turn when he brought in a little political context of the period, but that maybe he should develop those ideas further when he wrote up his presentation as a minipaper. He had raised an interesting question as to whether the whole Gold Rush episode had been a giant marketing scheme to get more people from the East and Midwest to make the trek across the country. But he should have been better prepared to answer the few probing questions that had come up. Ayni's questions were somewhat similar to those of her twin sister, also a student at Bay View. Her sister had first inquired about what made some people stop to settle the land along the way. Ayni knew her twin sister's method; her first question merely set the stage for what she really wanted to ask, which in this case had also been on Ayni's mind. How could Max bring in the political context without in some way addressing the whole issue of the displacement of the Indians and Mexicans, her sister had eventually challenged?

Finally, although Max's link between the Gold Rush forty-niners and the San Francisco Forty-Niners football team in terms of a certain kind of spirit was a nice touch, his attempt to extend the connection to his earlier marketing theme was, at best, strained. Mr. Clevelon would undoubtedly point this out to Max, who clearly wanted to be seen as a budding member of the C-Corps. Nevertheless, Ayni thought, this tendency of some students to strain the implications of the information they accessed was probably a good example of some of the misdirection that can come at times from leaving the classroom network and context to surf the various MOO environments on the global Internet to get into real-time electronic conversations with other users in order to get additional ideas on class topics. She wanted to share these comments with Max, but she wasn't sure it would all come out if she had to tell him face-to-face. And, she thought as she fought off a smile, he did have such a cute face. Mr. Clevelon insisted that all presentation responses be signed, so Max would still know which comments came from her. Some things just seemed easier to say or do electronically.

The original assignment had been given out at the start of class last Friday. Ayni remembered how she felt about getting more weekend homework. Mr. Clevelon had assigned each student to find a way to reveal something unique about the character of North Americans or to reveal an important aspect of what it meant to be a citizen of the United States by developing a presentation that emerged from or was somehow anchored to specific associations with the word "gold." He had gone on for a while explaining how, according to Vygotsky (who must be one of Mr. Clevelon's heroes from the air time his ideas got in the class) at least a single word is so saturated with "sense" that, at the level of what was called inner speech, it becomes concentrated with this notion of "sense" and as such stands for a complex of thoughts and feelings.

The students all knew, however, that the assignment had actually originated in a class discussion on Wednesday when they had gotten into a heated debate on what it meant at the dawn of the twenty-first century to be a U. S. citizen. Mr. Clevelon had initially meant for the focus of this class to be a discourse analysis of language differences in America. At Bay View, one criterion for each course offering was that its instructor present rationales for approval by the curriculum committees justifying how a course would contribute to student mastery of at least two of the five core Fundamental Literacies. Mr. Clevelon's North American Studies class was known throughout the school as a good primer for the current skills and subject-matter foci of the core courses in both culture and human development as well as language and communication(s).

Mr. Clevelon had pulled an old video documentary that had been done over a decade ago on Bay View and showed a scene in the discipline office where a white male teacher and a black male student were discussing an altercation they had had while a white male discipline officer mediated. Apparently, the teacher had grabbed the student to usher him out of an area where yet another problem was brewing, and the student had said something to the teacher regarding what might happen if the teacher touched him again. The teacher maintained that this was a threat, and there was (and continued to be) a clear and severe policy in the school regarding threatening a teacher. The student, however, argued that in street language this statement was actually a warning and not a threat. Despite the cogency of his argument, however, the student was still suspended.

The discussion of the video presentation would perhaps have re-mained focused at the level of language differences if Mr. Clevelon had not presented one more example of what he called "discourse styles in conflict" in preparation for his summation on strategies for negotiating diversity in meanings and perceptions. Another clip from the documen-tary showed a couple of white students and several students of color debating whether they considered themselves to be Americans. The class discussion, generated around this clip, moved well past the issues of language to an exploration of the thematic material itself. Someone had said that what America represented to many people was the hope of getting that pot of gold at the end of the rainbow. Someone else had countered that what America should represent was the hope of all the different colors of the rainbow interacting with each other, even as they remained distinct, revealing the dynamics and potential beauty of di-versity. Mr. Clevelon noted at this point in the discussion that these two ways of characterizing America were distinguished by perceptions of what some saw as the hoped-for *product* of being American in contrast to what others saw as a hoped for *process* of being American.

Mr. Clevelon had turned the point he was trying to make into a ques-tion. "Is America the rainbow, or is America the gold?" he asked. "Noth-ing Gold Can Stay," Ayni's sister had chimed in. "I know that line from somewhere," Max had said, almost to himself at first. "Didn't Ponyboy say that in that book *The Outsiders* by somebody named Hinton?" he continued, loud enough for the whole class to hear. He seemed happy that he had made the connection. "But it was originally the title of a poem by Robert Frost," Ayni's sister had answered with a slight smile. Someone else tried to tie the myth of King Midas into the discussion. When her fellow students had started throwing quotes around, Ayni remembered how she had brought in a point about *The Great Gatsby*, which she had read while in Chicago as an exchange student in Ms. Cato's class. She noted that the theme of that whole book had revolved around notions of the American Dream and that it also had images of gold strewn throughout the book, including the beginning quote that said something about wear a gold hat, if that will please her, which meant do anything you have to in order to attract the person of your dreams.

Anyway, Ayni was sure that it was this discussion specifically (more so than any of the Vygotsky stuff) that led to their homework assign-ment for the weekend. They were used to assignments being created in the moment, so to speak, by Mr. Clevelon, but what was different about this one was that he had asked students to work individually rather than assigning them to small groups like he did for most of their project/ presentations. This thought made Ayni recall what seemed to her like Mr. Clevelon's constant mouthing of his trite expression that students only had to master three things with information in order to do well in his class—access it, synthesize it (turn it into knowledge), and present it persuasively.

Ayni was supposed to be the next student to present, but Mr. Clevelon had yielded to students' request for a ten-minute break after Max finished. During the break, Ayni thought back to how she had initially gotten sidetracked into doing the assignment because the class's discussion had sparked her interest in seeing the entire documentary. It had been pretty long, but in the end she was glad she had taken the time to see it. On Saturday she had ridden her mountain bike out to the park at the marina and accessed the video through the school's library-net on her Pear 1. She wondered for a moment how people ever got any work done in the old days when they had to plug into a phone line to source any information that was not on their hard drive. When the video was over, she took off her head phones, snapped the color screen closed, and sat for some time looking at the bay and thinking. She was surprised by the fact that though a lot of things at Bay View had been very different over a decade ago, many things were still the same. More interestingly, she saw how the Bay View that she was attending now actually had grown out of the Bay View she had seen on the video.

Ayni knew all about the struggles to change Bay View that had happened in between because both her older brothers had graduated from there. She remembered her family's discussions around the dinner table about the various changes that were being instituted. It was interesting to actually see Ms. Parks on the video because her name had come up often in these discussions as one of the more vocal voices for the kinds of changes that gave Bay View its current form. Ayni had secretly hoped to take one of Ms. Parks' classes when she got to high school, but Ms. Parks had become Professor Parks after getting her Ph.D. in technology and instruction. She now worked over at the university training teachers.

The documentary made it clear how the heated discussions surrounding the de-tracking initiative foreshadowed the intense debates that brought Bay View's current curriculum and structure into existence. Ayni begin to review her own thinking about her choices of pathways through the variety of curriculum options. To graduate from Bay View, each student needed to complete a total of twenty units of credit. Each year-long class was one credit, and every student took five classes per year.

In addition to de-tracking classes, the frequency and duration of all classes had also been significantly changed to allow for extended collaboration on projects and more saturation with topics and issues. Three of the five classes for each student were Monday/Wednesday/Friday classes that met for two hours each. First period was from 8:00 a.m. to 10:00 a.m., with a half-hour break afterwards. Second period was from 10:30 a.m. to 12:30 p.m., with an hour for lunch break afterwards. Third period was from 1:30 p.m. to 3:30 p.m., after which on a couple of days each week a student would participate in either an intramural sports league or a selected mind/body awareness class. The two periods on Tuesday and Thursday were three hours each with an hour-and-a-half lunch break in between. Classes on these days also started at 8:00 a.m. and ended at 3:30 p.m. So, all five of a student's classes met for a total of six hours each week for the whole ten-month school year. The school site itself was always open until 6:00 p.m. After classes, students could use the school's resources to work on their projects or do other home-work, or socialize in defined areas. Often during this period, adults from the community and students from junior high schools came on campus to take part in various activities. All students had to take 25 percent of their total units in the five core requirement courses at some point dur-ing their four years in high school. However, this was where the simi-larities in student programs ended. Another 50 percent of course work was taken in a student-selected area of concentration. It was funny for Ayni to think of the term *student-selected* because these decisions were the consequences of the continual program-strategy meetings between students and their parents in conjunction with the students' teachers and counselors, which began back in junior high. Program strategies also included the selection of elective courses needed to complete the last 25 percent of credits needed for graduation.

This structure was originally suggested by a young faculty member who had graduated from one of the Ivy League schools. It was similar to the structure at his alma mater, and he and others had advocated that high school curricula should not be structured to prepare students for jobs, but to prepare them to be lifelong learners. These learners, they argued, should leave high school with the fundamental skills to access, analyze, synthesize, and interpret information as a foundation for the continual development of their abilities to make contributions to the knowledge base. These fundamental skills included systematic and ana-lytical thinking skills necessary for solving complex problems. In short, they argued, high school should provide an experience in which stu-dents learn to learn, and learn to love learning. They also argued that high school should be a place where students learned to live—with them-selves as individuals and with others through understanding themselves and their relationships to others.

The school's reformers had acknowledged that these were broad prin-ciples, but they were eventually translated into the core of Bay View's curriculum as the Five Fundamental Literacies: math and logic; science and technology; language and communication(s); culture and human development; and aesthetics and values. These were the only courses in the school's entire curriculum that were graded (all the others were pass/ no pass). The grade for the course was based on the final portfolio for each student that included a major project presentation/demonstration.

Each core course also culminated with its own Fundamental Literacy Exam (FLE) for which the highest possible score was 100 points. These exams were revised each year, and scaled in such a way that a score of 75 points or higher represented the upper echelons of excellence in the school—and in the country for that matter. To become a member of the 400 Club (having a combined total of 400 or more on the five exams) along with having high letter grades in at least four of the five core courses, was the standard for graduating with honors at Bay View. Members of the 400 Club were usually accepted at the best universities in the nation.

Each student had to take one Fundamental Literacy core course (and its end-of-semester exam) in her or his second year, two in the third year, and two in the fourth year. It was true that students would not know their final achievement levels for high school until early May of their fourth year, but college admission processes had adjusted to this timetable. Since final grades and scores were transferred instantly to each college that a student applied to, college admission decisions were able to be made known to students by mid-May. Additionally, more and more students were taking advantage of the year-long internship programs for high school graduates offered by the government, businesses, health organizations, community organizations, and the police and National Guard. Increasingly, colleges were encouraging applicants, even after early acceptance, to do an internship for a year rather than to go directly from high school to college. Universities had actually made getting either a one- or two-year internship or job a requirement for college graduates before granting them admission to graduate school.

At Bay View, there was no defined or necessary order in which core courses needed to be taken during the last three years of high school. In light of unique interests, strengths, and developmental needs, considerations of the best pathways through the curriculum for each student to maximize competencies in the Fundamental Literacies formed the essence of the ongoing program-strategy meetings between students and their parents and the school staff. The variety of possible approaches were the subjects of endless debates.

For faculty, the highest status and highest compensation that could be achieved in the school was to be elected and to work as a committee member for one of the Fundamental Literacy Curriculum Committees (FLCC) or the special committee on student Motivation, Instruction, and Assessment (MIA). The five FLCCs along with the MIA were charged with the intellectual and programmatic leadership of the school. FLCCs and the MIA each met once a month, but at each individual meeting there was always one representative present from each of the other FLCCs along with a representative from the MIA. When, for example, the five members of the Language and Communication(s) Committee met, they were joined by one member from the MIA along with one member from each of the other four FLCCs. The eleventh person present at each of these meetings was a member of the School Administration Committee (SAC). The chair of the SAC was roughly equivalent to what used to be called the school's principal. All eleven people, then, formed the total committee, and they each had an equal vote on all committee business of each individual committee. This structure allowed for continual cross-fertilization between the FLCCs, the MIA, and the SAC, and for a synthesis of the content and complexity of the FLEs.

Ayni knew all these details because her parents had dragged her and her sister to many of the meetings between school staff, parents, and student representatives at which these transformational decisions were being made while her brothers were going through high school. She remembered her mother being one of the main proponents for the intellectual and programmatic leadership of the school shifting away from the principal through the creation of the FLCCs. Her mother's argument was that no one person could possibly keep up with all the rapid changes in the various knowledge bases to which students needed to be exposed. It should be the faculty of the school, she reasoned, that should take leadership in these areas and that they should be appropriately compensated for doing so. This eventually gave rise to the SAC, and what was sought in its chairperson were skills as a master administrator. The first SAC chair had been a lawyer. The present one had a Master's degree in Business Administration.

The class break was coming to an end, and Ayni began to review her presentation in her mind. Her topic idea had come to her when, after seeing the video, she was just relaxing and watching a gorgeous sunset over the bay. To her left she saw the Bay Bridge which looked "like a huge prehistoric beast with tiny speckled insects buzzing along its curved back. . . . [T]he loading cranes on the edge of the east bay looked like giant horses, motionless and hypnotized. . . . [T]he Trans-America building rose out of downtown San Francisco demanding respect for its magnitude and aesthetics. In the middle of the bay, Alcatraz stood or rather slumped like an old man, warped and decayed by the passage of time

. . . . Rising behind this remnant . . . the Golden Gate Bridge, in all of her prestige and glory stood guard over the bay, beckoning in hope and pride, and everything bowed to her beauty."[1] With the ocean sunset profiling its splendor, Ayni realized that her topic had to be the Golden Gate Bridge.

Though it was starting to get dark, Ayni had clicked on her Pear 1 again to get information, first from the 90,000 K encyclopedia on her hard drive, whose citations included text, graphics, animation, and audio-video data; then from the school library; and, eventually, from the university and public library systems. She skimmed the encyclopedia text, but took more time studying the annotated bibliography it provided. A book entitled *Spanning the Gate,* a photo documentary with text by Stephen Cassady (1986), caught her interest as a source to start her thinking about her project. She found it in the public library system and loaded it onto her hard drive.

Ayni remembered getting all set to do a little reading when the "urgent message" light went on under her visual/voice prompt. She clicked to activate it even though she already knew who it would be. Her mother's face and voice boomed onto her screen. "You know how late it is, Ayni. Get yourself home, now!" Ayni did not have to bother to tell her mother where she was; her mom had already used the global locator in their home system to fix the exact position of her Pear 1 as her message was being received. Ayni knew she would have to try to explain why she had stayed at the marina so late. Though her parents would never say so, she knew they would also be thinking that this was something her sister would never do.

When Ayni was able to get back to her homework on Sunday, the idea of the Golden Gate Bridge as a symbol of something essential to being American was so rich that she wished she had more than one day to work on her project. Building the bridge seemed like an insurmountable challenge. Ayni learned from the Cassady text that the violent, pounding waters at the ocean entrance to the bay, where the largest underwater piers ever built had to be placed, were too menacing. Opponents argued that the Gate was too wide to be spanned by a suspension bridge. It would require the tallest towers and the longest, thickest cables ever made. But the biggest challenge was to convince the Bay Area counties to cooperate and financially support such an ambitious project in the midst of Depression bread lines and rampant unemployment.

Beyond the obvious symbol of connectedness latent in any image of bridges, Ayni thought that the story of the struggle to overcome these obstacles and create such a fine blend of art and function in a bridge generally considered to be the most beautiful in the world was a story that offered keen insights into the larger story of the United States in terms of both its problems and its possibilities. She had worked all day Sunday to design and complete her project which she hoped would show how the challenges of being a U. S. citizen required solving difficult problems to realize latent possibilities.

The students reassembled after the break while Ayni fought off her starting-gun anxiety. But unbelievably, Mr. Clevelon was calling on her sister to present next instead of her. Though they were twins, she and her sister did not really look very much alike, yet Mr. Clevelon was always confusing them. Her heart sank at the thought that they would probably run out of time and, if so, she would have to wait until Wednesday's class to present her work. The fact that this would give her an opportunity to make her presentation even better did not immediately comfort her. Max gave her a sympathetic glance; like everyone else except Mr. Clevelon, Max was aware of the mistake. But her sister was already confidently configuring the electronic infrastructure for her presentation.

Ayni now understood more about what it was that bothered her about Mr. Clevelon. He wasn't keenly enough aware of the uniqueness of each of his individual students. His good intentions toward all students masked the lack of a fine-tuned sensitivity to their distinctions. The digital audio system started cranking out stentorian sounds of cracking whips and horrifying screams. "Your name is Toby," a shrill voice commanded. The cacophony was disturbing. Her sister's presentation was on North American slavery. It was entitled "Black Gold."

Rewind

Elements in the above scenario contribute to a model of teaching and learning that attempts to address some of the challenges for new century schools. Some of these elements were seen in operation at various levels in the studies presented earlier. The scenario tries to illuminate possibilities for transforming classroom discourse and culture, but it also tries to illustrate a direction for change in the institutional structures and human relationships, change that is needed to facilitate reform in classroom interactions. So, after rewinding through key features from my studies that contribute to a model for teaching and learning in classrooms, I will also pause to consider implications for schoolwide structural changes that are suggested in the scenario.

The world of this scenario is not utopian. The problems that people have relating to one another, working together and against each other still exist. Ayni had unresolved concerns about Mr. Clevelon, Max, her sister, and her parents. The presence of greater technology, in and of itself, does not resolve these human concerns or other more specifically educational ones. Essentially, it is not merely the use of computers to mediate learning that is important; it is the efficacy of the pedagogical strategies themselves that makes the ultimate differences in the quality of student learning. Mr. Clevelon understood this point and reflected it in his notion that Pear 1's were "just a pound of information," but Ayni sensed that something more was yet possible in her learning experiences in Mr. Clevelon's class.

Mr. Clevelon and Ayni are imagined characters, but in the real-time life of classrooms, the problems of classroom discourse and culture are not fictional. From my investigations of language and social development taking place in the community sports setting, I speculated that some aspects of the communicative and behavioral interactions that had worked well for these youth had implications as well as correspondences to the school setting, and I have tried to show how they come into play in classrooms. The more global qualities had to do with strategies for general youth development, modeling specific skill development, instilling self-discipline in the players, policies for fair and equal participation for all players, and a policy of multiple coaches for each team. At the same time, the specific communicative interactions offered the youth a wide range of style options. These language styles were distinguished by being dialogical and receiver-centered, expressive and assertive, playful and colorful, as well as spontaneous and performative. It was also clear that features of these language uses were connected to some styles of discourse that are representative not just of African American youth, but youth generally.

In classrooms at Grand Crossing and Bay View high schools, and in the College Writing Program, I illustrated ways that many of these communicative and behavioral interactions were played out in schools. These settings revealed how integral teachers' roles were in creating the kinds of communicative and behavioral interactions that stimulated learning and skill development. These teachers were characterized in a number of ways as coaches, as mentors, as ethnographers, and implicitly as intellectuals. In Ms. Cato's classrooms, especially, she effectively played the role of mentor/coach. When learning was most fluid, the role of her students, like the role of the youth in the basketball league, was that of players, and classroom activities often reflected the structures of games.

In each of the studies, the key teachers who were focused on as examples of successful teaching also saw themselves functioning as coaches for their students. At the level of mentoring, they were each intensively engaged in relationship building. The nature of the classroom culture, and the caring and concern demonstrated by the teachers set the framework for a comfortable learning environment that helped to create a community of learners. These teachers' sense of their effectiveness was most often reflected in accomplishments and improvements made by their students, and consequently they saw themselves essentially on the same team as their students rather than separate from them.

Another important aspect was their role as models for both the student behaviors they wanted to elicit as well as for the work they were asking students to do. This last feature particularly helped students to clearly see ways to develop and practice their skills. Also of interest were ways in which teachers were able to respond to changes in the classroom environment on an immediate basis, the way coaches respond to new situations in games. Finally, their students were clearly comfortable using their own language in the classrooms for learning through talk strategies that were open, dialogical, and that honored and encouraged the students' emerging voices. The characterization of the student as player is not to denigrate that role of students in any way as nonserious, but rather identifies a certain amount of flexibility in the way students can operate in that role. All the justifications provided in the book for the power and value of various active learning strategies obtain here. When the classes were working well, students had more things that they could do actively such as projects, plays, presentations, and games. In *Harmonic Learning,* James Moffett (1992) provides an extensive, persuasive discussion of the value of organizing curricula around student projects, and in *Making the Grade,* Martin Covington (1992) gives extensive treatment to the value of organizing curricula around "serious games."

Looking at the classroom activities as game structures, in fact, further helped to create both flexibility and enjoyment in the strategies for learning. Properly designed, learning games were vehicles for organized discovery. Students learned collaboratively in teams and actively displayed their knowledge to one another through project/presentations, all within the context of ordered, rule-governed systems that had been built into their classrooms' discourse and culture by their teachers. The teamwork itself generated feelings of connectedness among students across some of the borders that existed in diverse classrooms. Competition was present, but it had a different result as competition between teams. It actually contributed to more sophisticated levels of collaboration within teams as well as appreciation for the work of other teams. In fact, what happens in the game of learning is better characterized as challenge rather than competition because in order for the activity to be challenging all participants have to cooperate at high levels. These things taken together were key strategies that allowed the successful teachers in the various studies in this book to make viable connections between streets and schools through the engaging nature of their pedagogy and curriculum. I have also noted from these studies how their students' engagement in learning was intricately tied to issues of individual and group identity and representation.

These issues were foregrounded with a futuristic twist in the teaching and learning depicted in Mr. Clevelon's class. His coaching/ mentoring/teaching approach rippled throughout the school generally through the C-Corps and the Warrior-Poets Society. Overall, despite Ayni's mixed feelings about him, his personal involvement with students and caring about their lives beyond the classroom is the most important consideration that a coaching/mentoring perspective provides. In an article entitled "What a Coach Can Teach a Teacher," Roland Tharp and Ronald Gallimore (1976) analyze the coaching/teaching style of John Wooden, the greatest college basketball coach of all time, and note that "Wooden also went beyond basketball to work with players on their personal problems and careers" (p. 76). They reinforce this point with Wooden's comments on voice from his autobiography: "I often tell my players that next to my own flesh and blood, they are the closest to me. They are my children. I get wrapped up in them, their lives and their problems" (p. 77).

Mr. Clevelon's class itself revolved around collaborative projects that culminated in performative, multimedia presentations and minipapers, even though the project described was done individually by students. Emphasizing presentation, he clearly required that his students' learning be both active and integrative. The potential for excitement in learning was supplied by the students themselves in the dynamic, multimedia events in which they presented the knowledge they had acquired. Yet, this excitement was also designed into Mr. Clevelon's pedagogy and curriculum in the strategies he used for discussions and for motivating the students' independent investigations. His modeling and motivation efforts provided springboards for the leaps of imagination he required of his students. And his project assignments allowed elbow room for representation of the unique concerns and issues that flowed from the variety of lived experiences and interests of each of his students. Max was able to bring in his interests in sports; Ayni's sister was able to connect issues from a historical/political context; and Ayni was able to explore her concerns for the problems and possibilities in creating a major work of functional beauty. In so doing, these students were actively co-creating the curriculum's content, and through their presentations, they themselves used teaching to learn.

Mr. Clevelon had a curriculum plan for the week, but his pedagogical style was adaptable enough to take advantage of the spontaneous direction that the discussion had taken from his video prompts such that the actual assignment that emerged for the weekend was quite different from what he had initially planned. This, perhaps, exemplified the workings of a mutable curriculum and pedagogy for teaching it that will more and more be a requirement of new century schooling. To be sure, some of the plasticity needed will be greatly facilitated by new technological capacities, but this capacity alone is virtually dormant until it is brought to life in effective pedagogical strategies like these that have been highlighted.

As depicted, Mr. Clevelon was an effective new century school teacher, but as Ayni correctly sensed, part of a teacher's ultimate effectiveness goes beyond good intentions and beyond sensitivity to generalized cultural categories. Mr. Clevelon was not aware that Ayni felt she had been treated unfairly, and he needed to develop a more finely tuned perception of the uniqueness, needs, and strengths of each individual student in his class. Such a notion sees the teacher as ethnographer; each student is thus an informant in the study and development of individual distinctions in learning.

Pause

The scenario of a possible Bay View High School suggested schoolwide structural changes that are not reflected in the studies discussed in this book. Possibilities for new structures were presented in this chapter because it is important to understand that transformations at the classroom level, in order to be optimally effective, must operate in a schoolwide context that is not just supportive but integrally linked to new strategies for teaching and learning. Teachers like Ms. Parks and Ms. Cato routinely circumvented administration-imposed obstacles to the kind of teaching that they knew was necessary to reach their students. But it is not enough merely for individual teachers to have found ways to be successful. For schools to meet the challenges of the future, real reforms will have to be comprehensive and systemic. Schools must be tightly structured, orderly, and efficient, and yet they must be flexible enough to incorporate improvisation and change. Perhaps most important, schools will need to develop mechanisms that honor and reward teachers as intellectuals who are responsible for the shape and scope of pedagogy, curriculum, and assessment in the school.

The Bay View scenario offered a number of considerations for a new century school structure. It was directed toward achieving standards of excellence while simultaneously permitting considerable flexibility in approaches to achieve these standards through core requirements, areas of concentration, and elective courses, along with significantly restructured class schedules and class-period time. The viability of these structures turned on the axis of empowerment of teachers. Administrators were seen as facilitators of these teachers' curriculum designs.

The subject areas themselves were significantly changed. For example, in the place of four years of English, the school had a core requirement for fundamental literacy in language and communication(s). Students were given a foundation in American and world literatures, but the focus of their fundamental literacy in this area depended on developing competency in and understanding the issues and problems of language and communication. A number of researchers have argued for removing literature from the center of the secondary school English curriculum in favor of a more specific study of language and communication. Yagelski (1992), for example, notes that "we should use literature as an opportunity to teach students about language and language use—and about the complicated connections among different forms of language, including literary language, and the social, political, economic, and cultural contexts out of which it grows" (p. 31).

In the scenario I described, the five curriculum committees along with the Committee on Motivation, Instruction, and Assessment established the intellectual direction and content of learning for the entire school. It was important to have a special committee for issues of teaching that cuts across all of the curriculum committees. On this committee, motivation had its place in front of instruction and assessment. These school leadership committees were also structured to allow for extensive cross-fertilization. The fact the Fundamental Literacy Exams were revised each year implied that the understanding of what was fundamental for students to know was itself in a constant state of revision in response to the continued creation of new knowledge. Of course, for any of this to work the teachers themselves would have to be properly trained, motivated, and compensated to achieve a new vision of their role and work in school.

The scenario also suggested that students had a valuable voice and vote in the process through which individual teachers became leaders in the school. Structures were in place for students to evaluate their teachers even as they were evaluated by their teachers. Provisions for the students' education to go beyond the boundaries of the local school were reflected in the extensiveness of student exchange programs, internships, and computer networking. Parents, too, were characterized as needing to be intimately involved in the school's ongoing transformations. And, there were hints of the existence of increased community involvement both as contributor to and as recipient of the resources of the school, whose site remained open and hospitable well past the end of classes each day. The school site had become a community resource.

The ultimate viability of teaching and learning in individual classrooms is linked to the institutional and programmatic structures of the entire school. And clearly, schools themselves must be understood within a larger socioeconomic and political context. Still, teachers have considerable agency to transform life and learning in schools, and we understand that meaningful change also means changing ourselves. To clarify our aims for future schooling, we acknowledge how possibilities and problems are rooted in the past and present. Yet, in shooting for excellence, we also find our focus on two targets simultaneously, and both are constantly moving. One is cultural diversity; the other is cultural change. Education provides one of our best hopes for understanding and appreciating diversity and change. But we must learn better ways to build on diversity, to manage change, and to keep cultural worlds from drifting apart. Citizens of the twenty-first century are being educated right now. The challenge of new century schools is to teach them knowledge, skills, and values to collectively create rainbows of productive, nonoppressive human interactions that increase the prospects of individuals finding their personal gold.

Note

1. This quoted text comes from the student essay entitled "Stentorian Man," which was assessed in Chapter 3.

Works Cited

Abrahams, R. D. (1976). *Talking black*. Rowley, MA: Newbury.

Abrahams, R. D. (1989). Black talking on the streets. In R. Bauman & J. Sherzer (Eds.), *Explorations in the ethnography of speaking* (pp. 243–265). Cambridge: Cambridge University Press.

Alexander, D. (1994, September 7). Critical beatdown: The culture clash between rappers and hip-hop writers erupts into violence. *San Francisco Bay Guardian*, p. 28.

Alpert, B. (1991). Student's resistance in the classroom. *Anthropology & Education Quarterly, 22*, 350–366.

Anderson, G. L. & Irvine, P. (1993). Informing critical literacy with ethnography. In C. Lankshear & P. L. McLaren (Eds.), *Critical literacy: Politics, praxis, and the postmodern* (pp. 81–104). New York: State University of New York Press.

Anderson, S. K. (1990). The effect of athletic participation on the academic aspirations and achievement of African American males in a New York City high school. *Journal of Negro Education, 59*(3), 507–516.

Andrews, S.,Olsson, S., & Robinson-Odomfirst, I. M. (1994, October 18). *School Colors* [Film]. Public Broadcasting Station.

Applegate, J. et al. (Eds.). (1970). *Adventures in world literature*. New York: Harcourt Brace Jovanovich.

Aronowitz, S. & Giroux, H. A. (1991). *Postmodern education: Politics, culture, and social criticism*. Minneapolis: University of Minnesota Press.

Bakhtin, M. (1986). *Speech genres and other late essays*. (V. W. McGee, Trans.). In C. Emerson & M. Holquist (Eds.). Austin: University of Texas Press.

Banks, J. A. (1991). A curriculum for empowerment, action, and change. In C. Sleeter (Ed.), *Empowerment through multicultural education* (pp. 125–141). Albany, NY: State University of New York Press.

Banks, J. A. (1993). The canon debate, knowledge construction, and multicultural education. *Educational Researcher, 22*(5), 4–14.

Bassey, M. (1989). Does action research require sophisticated research methods. In D. Hustler, A. Cassidy, & E. C. Cuff (Eds.), *Action research in classrooms and schools* (pp. 18–24). London: Allen & Unwin.

Bauman, R. (Ed.). (1992). *Folklore, cultural performances, and popular entertainments*. New York: Oxford University Press.

Bauman, R. & Sherzer, J. (Eds.). (1989). *Explorations in the ethnography of speaking*. 2nd edition. Cambridge: Cambridge University Press.

Bloom, H. (1987). *The closing of the American mind: How higher education has failed democracy and impoverished the souls of today's students*. New York: Simon & Schuster.

Braddock, H. (1980). Race sport and social mobility: A critical review. *Sociological Symposium, 30*(1), 18–38.

Braddock, H., et al. (1991). Bouncing back: Sports and academic resilience among African American males. *Education and Urban Society, 24*(1), 113–131.

Brooks, C. (Ed.). (1985). *Tapping potential: English and language arts for the black learner.* Urbana, IL: National Council of Teachers of English.

Carroll, E. J. (1994, June). Hip-hop honkies in the heartland. *Esquire,* 102.

Cassady, S. (1979). *Spanning the gate: The Golden Gate Bridge.* Mill Valley: Squarebooks.

Cazden, C. B. (1988). *Classroom discourse: The language of teaching and learning.* Portsmouth: Heinemann.

Cintron, R. (1993). Wearing a pith helmet at a sly angle, or, can writing researchers do ethnography in a postmodern era? *Written Communication, 10*(3), 371–412.

Collins, E. C. & Green, J. L. (1990). Metaphors: The construction of a perspective. *Theory into Practice, 29,*(2), 71–77.

Cone, J. (1992, May). Untracking advanced placement English: Creating opportunity is not enough. *Phi Delta Kappan.*

Conroy, P. (1986). *The prince of tides.* Boston: Houghton Mifflin.

Coupland, D. (1991). *Generation X: Tales for an accelerated culture.* New York: St. Martin's Press.

Covington, M. (1992). *Making the grade: A self-worth perspective on motivation and school reform.* Cambridge: Cambridge University Press.

Dawkins, M. (1982). Sports and mobility aspirations among black male college students. *Journal of Social and Behavioral Sciences, 28,* 77–81.

Delain, M. T., Pearson, P. D., & Anderson, R. C. (1985). Reading comprehension and creativity in black language use: You stand to gain by playing the sounding game. *American Educational Research Association Journal, 22,* 155–173.

Delpit, L. (1988). The silenced dialogue: Power and pedagogy in educating other people's children. *Harvard Educational Review, 58*(3), 280–298.

Delpit, L. (1990). Language diversity and learning. In S. Hynds, & D. L. Rubin (Eds.), *Perspectives on talk and learning* (pp. 247–266). Urbana, IL: National Council of Teachers of English.

Delpit, L. (1991). A conversation with Lisa Delpit. *Language Arts, 68,* 541–547.

Dillon, D. (1985). The dangers of computers in literacy education: Who's in charge here? In D. Chandler & S. Marcus (Eds.), *Computers and literacy* (pp. 86–107). Philadelphia: Open University Press.

Dyson, M. (1993). *Reflecting black: African-American cultural criticism.* Minneapolis: University of Minnesota Press.

Ebony Man. (1992, March). Vol. 2, No. 3.

Edwards, H. (1973). *Sociology of sport.* Homewood, IL: The Dorsey Press.

Ellsworth, E. (1994). Representation, self-representation, and the meanings of difference: Questions for educators. In R. A. Martusewicz & W. M. Reynolds (Eds.), *Inside/out: Contemporary critical perspectives in education* (pp. 99–108). New York: St. Martin's Press.

Epic of Gilgamesh, The. (1970). In Applegate, J., et al. (Eds.), *Adventures in world literature.* New York: Harcourt Brace Jovanovich.

Evans, W. H. & Walker, J. L. (1966). *New trends in the teaching of English in secondary schools.* Chicago: Rand McNally.

Farrell, E. (1988). Giving voice to high school students: Pressure and boredom: 'Ya know what I'm saying?' *American Educational Research Journal, 25,* 489–502.

Ferdman, B. M. (1990). Literacy and cultural identity. *Harvard Educational Review, 60*(2), 181–204.

Fernandes, J. V. (1988). From the theories of cultural and social reproduction to the theory of resistance. *British Journal of Sociology of Education, 9*(2), 169–180.

Fine, G. (1979). Small groups and culture creation: The ideoculture of Little League baseball teams. *American Sociological Review, 44,* 733–745.

Fine, G. (1987). *With the boys: Little League Baseball and preadolescent culture.* Chicago: University of Chicago Press.

Fine, G. & Mechling, J. (1993). Child saving and children's cultures at century's end. In Heath & McLaughlin (Eds.), *Identity and inner-city youth: Beyond ethnicity and gender* (pp.120–146). New York: Teachers College Press.

Flower, L. & Hayes, J. R. (1981). A cognitive process theory of writing. *College Composition and Communication, 32*(4), 365–387.

Fordham, S. & J. Ogbu. (1986). Black students' school success: Coping with the burden of "acting white." *The Urban Review, 18,* 176–206.

Freedman, S. W., et al. (1987). *Research in writing: Past, present, and future* (Tech. Rep. No. 1). Berkeley: Center for the Study of Writing, University of California.

Freire, P. (1970). *Pedagogy of the oppressed.* New York: Herder and Herder.

Freire, P. (1986). *Education for critical consciousness.* New York: Continuum.

Gates, H. L. Jr. (1988). *The signifying monkey: A theory of African-American literary criticism.* New York: Oxford University Press.

Gates, H. L. Jr. (1992). *Loose canons.* New York: Oxford University Press.

Gates, H. L. Jr. (1993). Beyond the culture wars: Identities in dialogue. *Profession,* 93–98.

Gates, H. L. Jr. (1995). Thirteen ways of looking at a black man. *The New Yorker, 23,* 56–65.

Gee, J. P. (1989). The narrativization of experience in the oral style. *Journal of Education, 171*(1), 75–96.

Gee, J. P. (1995). Learning and reading: The situated sociocultural mind. Paper presented at the annual convention of the National Council of Teachers of English, San Diego, California.

Giroux, H. (1983). Theories of reproduction and resistance in the new sociology of education: A critical analysis. *Harvard Educational Review, 53*(3), 257–293.

Giroux, H. A. & Simon, R. I. (1989). *Popular culture: Schooling and everyday life.* New York: Bergin and Garvey.

Gilroy, P. (1993). *The black Atlantic: Modernity and double consciousness.* Cambridge, MA: Harvard University Press.

Goodlad, J. (1984). *A place called school: Prospects for the future.* New York: McGraw Hill Book Company.

Grimshaw, A. D. (1990). *Conflict talk: Sociolinguistic investigations of arguments in conversations.* Cambridge: Cambridge University Press.

Gumperz, J. (1982). *Discourse strategies.* Cambridge: Cambridge University Press.

Haas, C. (1996). *Writing technology: Studies on the materiality of literacy.* Mahwah, NJ: L. Erlbaum Associates.

Hall, S. (1993). What is this 'black' in black popular culture? *Social Justice, 20* (1–2), 104–114.

Hammersley, M. (1986). Introduction. *Controversies in classroom research.* Philadelphia: Open University Press.

Harris, O. & Hunt, L. (1982). Race and sports involvement: Some implications of athletics for black and white youth. *Journal of Social and Behavioral Sciences, 28*(3), 95–103.

Heath, S. B. (1982). Protean shapes in literacy events: Ever-shifting oral and literate traditions. In D. Tannen, (Ed.), *Spoken and written language: Exploring orality and literacy* (pp. 91–117). Norwood, NJ: Ablex.

Heath, S. B. (1983). *Ways with words: Language life and work in communities and classrooms.* Cambridge: Cambridge University Press.

Heath, S. B. (1987). Foreword. In H. J. Graff (Ed.), *Labyrinths of literacy.* Cambridge: Cambridge University Press.

Heath, S. B. (1991). It's about winning! The language of knowledge in baseball. In L. B. Resnick, J. M. Levine & S. B. Teasley (Eds.), *Perspectives on socially shared cognition* (pp. 101–124). Washington, DC: American Psychological Association.

Heath, S. B. & Branscombe, A. (1985). "Intelligent writing" in an audience community: Teacher, students, and researcher. In S. W. Freedman (Ed.), *The acquisition of written language: Response and revision* (pp. 3–32). Norwood, NJ: Ablex.

Heath, S. B. & Langman, J. (1994). Shared thinking and the register of coaching. In D. Biber & E. Finegan (Eds.), *Sociolinguistic perspectives on register* (pp. 82–105). New York: Oxford University Press.

Heath, S. B. & McLaughlin, M. W. (1987). Language, socialization, and neighborhood-based organizations: Moving youth beyond dependency on school and family. Proposal submitted to the Spenser Foundation.

Heath, S. B. & McLaughlin, M. W. (Eds.). (1993). *Identity and inner-city youth: Beyond ethnicity and gender.* New York: Teachers College Press.

Hirsch, E. D. (1987). *Cultural literacy: What every American needs to know.* Boston: Houghton Mifflin.

hooks, b. (1994). *Teaching to transgress: Education as the practice of freedom.* New York: Routledge.

Hymes, D. (1974). *Foundations in sociolinguistics: An ethnographic approach.* Philadelphia: University of Pennsylvania Press.

Jones, R. (1994, November 29). Fun and games can go a long way for kids. *The Daily Californian,* p. 20.

Knapp, M. S. with Adelman, N.E., et al.(1995). *Teaching for meaning in high-poverty classrooms.* New York: Teachers College Press.

Kochman, T. (1981). *Black and white in conflict.* Chicago: University of Chicago Press.

Kochman, T. (1983). The boundary between play and nonplay in black verbal dueling. *Language and Society, 12,* 330.

Ladson-Billings, G. (1990). Culturally relevant teaching: Effective instruction for black students. *The College Review, 155,* 20–25.

Ladson-Billings, G. (1994). *The dreamkeepers: The successful teachers of African American children.* San Francisco: Jossey-Bass.

Lee, C. D. (1991). Big picture talkers/words walking without masters: The instructional implications of ethnic voices for an expanded literacy. *Journal of Negro Education, 60*(3), 291–304.

Light, A. (1994). The man who won't be Prince. *Vibe, 2*(3), 45–50.

Lomotey, K. (1990). *Going to school: The African-American experience.* New York: State University of New York Press.

Lunsford, A. A., Moglen, H. & Slevin, J. (Eds.). (1990). Introduction. *The right to literacy.* New York: The Modern Language Association.

Mahiri, J. (1991). Discourse in sports: Language and literacy features of preadolescent African American males in a youth basketball program. *Journal of Negro Education, 60*(3), 305–313.

Mailer, N. (1957). The white Negro. San Francisco: City Lights Books.

Mehan, H., Hertweck, A., Combs, S. E., & Flynn, P.J. (1992). Teacher's interpretations of students' behaviors. In L. C. Wilkinson (Ed.), *Communicating in the Classroom* (pp. 297–321). New York: Academic Press.

Mitchell-Kernan, C. (1971). *Language behavior in a black urban community.* Berkeley, CA: Language Behavior Research Laboratory, University of California at Berkeley.

Moffett, J. (1983). *Teaching the universe of discourse.* Boston: Houghton Mifflin.

Moffett, J. (1992). *Harmonic learning: Keynoting school reform.* Portsmouth, NH: Heinemann.

Morrison, T. (1992). *Playing in the dark: Whiteness and the literary imagination.* Cambridge, MA: Harvard University Press.

Ninety percent of public school teachers white, national study finds. (1996, October 17). *The San Francisco Chronicle,* p. A2.

Nolan, R. (1994). *Cognitive practices: Human language and human knowledge.* Oxford: Blackwell.

Oakes, J. (1985). *Keeping track: How schools structure inequality.* New Haven: Yale University Press.

Our Daily Work. (1993, October–November). *Dorothy Day House Newsletter.*

Pennycook, A. (1995). English in the world/the world in English. In J. W. Tollefson (Ed.), *Power and inequality in language education* (pp. 34–58). New York: Cambridge University Press.

Perl, S. (1979). The composing processes of unskilled college writers. *Research in the Teaching of English, 13*(4), 317–336.

Picou, J. S. (1978). Race, athletic achievement and educational aspiration. *Sociological Quarterly, 19,* 429–438.

Powell, C. T. (1991). Rap music: An education with a beat from the street. *Journal of Negro Education, 60*(3), 246–247.

Rahlman, R. K. (1993, August 25). Take my shtick . . . please: Is live comedy dying? *The Bay Guardian,* p. 24.

Reed, R. J. (1988). Education and achievement of young black males. In Gibbs & J. Taylor (Eds.), *Young, black, and male in America: An endangered species* (pp. 37–96). Dover: Auburn Housing Publishing Company.

Reich, R. (1991). *The work of nations: Preparing ourselves for 21st century capitalism.* New York: Knopf.

Rose, M. (1989). *Lives on the boundary: The struggles and achievements of America's unprepared.* New York: Penguin Books.

Rose, M. (1995). *Possible lives: The promise of public education in America.* New York: Penguin Books.

Sa'di. (1970). The manners of kings. In J. Applegate et al. (Eds.), *Adventures in world literature* (pp. 340–341). New York: Harcourt Brace Jovanovich Publishers.

Saville-Troike, M. (1989). *The ethnography of communication: An introduction.* New York: Basil Blackwell.

Schatz, Howard. (1993). *Homeless: Portraits of Americans in hard times.* San Francisco: Chronicle Books.

Scribner, S. & Cole, M. (1981). *The psychology of literacy.* Cambridge, MA: Harvard University Press.

Sizer, T. (1984). *Horace's compromise: The dilemma of the American high school.* Boston: Houghton Mifflin.

Skow, J. (1993, April 5). General Patton, sit down and shut up! *Time, 141,* 68.

Sleeter, C. E. & Grant, C. (Eds.). (1991). Mapping terrains of power: Student cultural knowledge versus classroom knowledge. *Empowerment through multicultural education.* Albany: State University of New York Press.

Snyder, E. E. & Spreitzer, E. (1990). High school athletic participation as related to college attendance among black, Hispanic, and white males. *Youth and Society, 21*(3), 390–398.

Street, B. (1984). *Literacy in theory and practice.* Cambridge: Cambridge University Press.

Street, B. (Ed.). (1993). *Cross-cultural approaches to literacy.* Cambridge: Cambridge University Press.

Style, E. (1992). The AAUW Report: How schools shortchange girls. *The American Association of University Women Report, 372.* AAUW and National Education Association. New York: Marlowe and Company.

Tan, A. (1989). *The joy luck club.* New York: Putnam.

Tharp, R. G. & Gallimore, R. (1976, January). What a coach can teach a teacher. *Psychology Today,* 76–77.

Tharp, R. G., & Gallimore, R. (1988). *Rousing minds to life: Teaching, learning, and schooling in social context.* Cambridge: Cambridge University Press.

Tully, S. (1994, April 4). The universal teenager. *Fortune, 129,* 14.

Vygotsky, L. (1986). Thought and language (Rev. ed.). Cambridge, MA: MIT Press.

Walker, A. (1982). *The color purple*. New York: Simon & Schuster, Inc.

West, C. (1990). The new cultural politics of difference. In Ferguson, R., et al. (Eds.), *Out there: Marginalization and contemporary cultures* (pp. 19–36). Cambridge, MA: MIT Press in association with the New Museum of Contemporary Art.

West, C. (1993a). *Race matters*. Boston: Beacon Press.

West, C. (1993b, September). Interview by James Ledbetter. *Vibe, 1* (1).

Yagelski, R. P. (1992). Literature and literacy: Rethinking English as a school subject. *English Journal, 83*, 30–36.

Index

Author

Photograph: Jelani K. Mahiri

Jabari Mahiri is assistant professor of education in the division of language, literacy, and culture at the University of California at Berkeley. His research focuses on strategies of reform in the teaching and learning of urban youth with a specific emphasis on writing development. He taught high school for seven years in the Chicago Public Schools and has supervised student teachers and mentored new teachers. He was also the first chair of the Board of Directors for New Concept School, an alternative school for African American children that has been in existence for twenty-one years. Mahiri is completing two new books, *Stepping Out-of-Bounds: When Scholarship Athletes Become Academic Scholars* and *What They Don't Learn in School: Literacy in the Lives of Urban Youth.*

This book was set in Palatino by Electronic Imaging.
Typeface used on the cover was Univers.
The book was printed on 60-lb. Williamsburg offset paper by Versa Press.